More Praise for *Finding Reality*

The 21st century is going to require skilled decisions more than ever before. As we face the possibility of sending astronauts to Mars, deal with the myriad of issues that relate to our fragile Earth, how can we know that the decisions we make are the most appropriate? In *Finding Reality: Four Ways of Knowing*, Dr. Olson offers a very useful tool that politicians, business leaders, educators, among others can use to assist them reach those very skilled decisions.

> **—R. Lynn Bondurant, Ph.D., Education Officer (Retired), NASA Glenn Research Center**

Dr Olson uses his creativity and thirst for the provocative to blend together many concepts and has thus developed a different way of exploring how we know what we know. He provides a very different way of thinking about how knowledge is used by each unique individual and that is why this book is such a treasure. I truly believe that Ed has opened the door for individuals to not only understand what drives their own perspectives of the world but also a way to understand how others perceive the world the way they do. This is a must read if you are to be meaningfully engaged in today's multi-cultural environment.

> **—Kristine Quade, Ed.D., JD**

Reality. The idea of Reality reminds me of the story of the blind men and the elephant. Four wise, blind men were tasked with describing an elephant. One felt a leg, one felt the side, one felt the tail and the last felt the trunk. What ensued was an argument about what the Reality of an elephant is. It is like a wall! It is like a rope! It is like a snake! It is like a tree! Dr. Olson's book makes sense of the multitude of ways that we each perceive reality and helps us to understand ourselves and the other souls we encounter on life's journey.

> **—Mary Ann Whalen, LCSW, Psychotherapist**

I highly recommend the Ways of Knowing Model for any company that is trying to better understand how customers think about their product. The model not only helps you understand how others think, it also provides clues to actions that you can take to change their opinion. When we used this framework at Float, it helped us prioritize our marketing strategy to focus on consumers' reliance on "Authority" in making financial decisions. At Float, we have the "Empiricism", "Insight" and "Praxis" ways of knowing on our side. The numbers show that interest is dangerous, people intuitively feel bad when they owe compounding interest, and when people try Float they love it. Our challenge is with "Authority." Credit card companies create their own type of powerful authority by spending billions of dollars on advertising. After several generations of these ads, consumers have come to believe that credit cards are the best way to borrow money, notwithstanding what they know to be true from "Empiricism", "Insight" and "Praxis." Going through this Ways of Knowing analysis helped us understand that we need to focus on using "Authority" in our marketing by, for example, seeking the endorsements of high profile personal finance commentators and countering the influence of credit cards through blogs, word of mouth, humor, etc.

—**Shane Hadden, CEO, FloatMoney. LLC**

"What is real?" Ed Olson has provided us with a holistic approach to help us in our search for reality. Not only do we find reality through scientific analysis, but also through intuition, not only by philosophical/theological study, but by silently letting the divine within us speak. Whether you are a thinker or a meditator, *Finding Reality: Four Ways of Knowing* will be helpful in your everyday life journey. I wholeheartedly recommend it.

— **Rev. Cliff Lawrence, UCC Clergy**

Why should I want to know more? Because the innate demand to know more will persist. **So What?** Use the Ways of Knowing Model to make sense of all information that can be considered when addressing a question and develop confidence in the "truth" that emerges. **Now What?** Using the model and the knowledge that emerges, positions one to discern what action to take — how to live with purpose.

—**Judith Frye, Wisconsin Public Administrator (Retired)**

This is a wisdom book for 21st century seekers of truth and for organizations that need to change. In an age of polarization, when hard-headed empiricists often clash with soft-headed intuitives in a common search for truth and concrete solutions to our problems, here is a book that identifies and honors multiple ways of knowing reality. Using down-to-earth examples, the reader is skillfully and expertly guided through ways of knowing which, when brought to bear on our personal and corporate life situations, results in creative emergence—the surprising solution that is born when intuition, facts, inherited wisdom, and practice converge. I highly recommend this book.

—**Bruce Sanguin, Author of *If Darwin Prayed and Darwin, Divinity, and the Dance of the Cosmos***

A well written and easy read for a deep subject — knowing. Ed Olson provides us with a map to guide our way through the puzzle of "knowing" with tools to help us understand our way of knowing. I loved reading this book and will read it over many times.

—**Emily Axelrod, The Axelrod Group.**

FINDING
Reality

FINDING *Reality*

Four Ways of Knowing

EDWIN E. OLSON, PhD

Foreword by Glenda H. Eoyang

ARCHWAY
PUBLISHING

Archway Publishing books may be ordered through booksellers or by contacting:

Archway Publishing
1663 Liberty Drive
Bloomington, IN 47403
www.archwaypublishing.com
1-(888)-242-5904

Because of the dynamic nature of the Internet, any web addresses or links contained in this book may have changed since publication and may no longer be valid. The views expressed in this work are solely those of the author and do not necessarily reflect the views of the publisher, and the publisher hereby disclaims any responsibility for them.

Bible quotations are from *The Message*, Copyright © 2011 by Eugene Peterson.

Photos have been purchased from Depositphotos.com

Excerpts from *Adaptive Action: Leveraging Uncertainty in Your Organization* (2013) are reproduced with permission from Glenda H. Eoyang and Royce J. Holladay, HSD Institute.

Any people depicted in stock imagery provided by Thinkstock are models, and such images are being used for illustrative purposes only. Certain stock imagery © Thinkstock.

ISBN: 978-1-4808-1239-0 (sc)
ISBN: 978-1-4808-1240-6 (e)

Library of Congress Control Number: 2014919009

Printed in the United States of America.

Archway Publishing rev. date: 11/21/2014

To Rev. Walter Fohs, Rev. Becky Robbins-Penniman, and Marilyn Bowman, whose openness, courage, and generosity of spirit have helped me and many at the Lamb of God Lutheran-Episcopal Church in Fort Myers, Florida, seek our own ways of knowing truth.

Real knowledge should be such knowledge that connects man to his
home in the cosmos and also to his purpose on this earth.
Hakan Snellman, Swedish physicist

Take your mess and find a message.
Alan Jones, Dean Emeritus, Grace Cathedral of the Episcopal Diocese of California

One-sidedness is an attitude that always favors one way of feeling or
acting especially without considering any other possibilities.
Merriam-Webster dictionary

The world keeps happening, in accordance with its rules; it's
up to us to make sense of it and give it a value.
Sean Carroll, theoretical physicist

It ain't what you don't know that gets you into trouble. It's
what you know for sure that just ain't so.
Mark Twain and Charles Kettering

Contents

List of Figures and Tables

Foreword

In times of uncertainty, answers have a very short shelf-life, but a good question can last a lifetime.

When I began working with chaos theory and complexity science in the late 1980s, I was looking for guidance in an unpredictable business environment. A bright friend asked, "If a science doesn't help you predict and control the future, then why would you study it?" I mumbled something about unpredictable futures being much more interesting than predictable ones. Since then, wise action in uncertainty has become more than just interesting, it is urgent. Economic, weather, social, and political climates have become so unstable that we expect surprise in all parts of our private and public lives. In many facets of decision making and action taking, the lessons of chaos have proven to be practical guides to success in an uncertain future.

Chief among the lessons of complexity is the power of inquiry.

As thinking, responsible human beings, we use our memories, imaginations, and in-the-moment perceptions to collect data, make meaning, and take action. It is just what humans do. When change is slow and predictable, our assumptions give us answers and reality confirms our beliefs. When change is fast and unpredictable, assumptions can lead us astray. Only questions give us the power to see, understand, and influence change that is radically unpredictable. Inquiry becomes the primary survival strategy in times of chaos and uncertainty.

In chaotic environments we cannot predict what will happen, so we have to ask. Boundaries shift, so we ask about the range of influence. Unknowable factors influence the path of change, so we ask about what differences make a difference. Relationships are complicated and transient, so we ask what networks need to be created or destroyed. It is impossible to know what will happen with any degree of certainty, so we stand in inquiry and prepare to adapt.

Ed Olson has provided a map to guide inquiry for personal growth and development in uncertain times. The models and methods he shares inspire wise individual action and collaborative efforts. He presents tools for thought and action to support us all as we ask: What do I know and how do I know it? What choices do I create for myself and others? Now what will I do to fulfill my personal purpose?

Drawing from a wide range of human systems dynamics, scientific, psychological, philosophical, and religious sources, Ed builds a map that is both practical and inspiring. The stories he shares bring the ways of knowing to life. The reflective questions and assessments connect the ways of knowing to personal choices and decision making. The frames he builds inform adaptive action and support the emerging patterns of thought, relationship, and action.

Ed's map is a powerful guide, but it is not an answer. Like any useful tool in an emergent reality, it is a source of ever more stimulating questions. As I read it, I was inspired by questions that can last a lifetime, even while I know that today's answers will be obsolete tomorrow. I expect that others will find here confirmation of their experience and inspiration to inquire into a future they can create.

Glenda H. Eoyang, PhD
Executive Director
Human Systems Dynamics Institute

June, 2014

Preface

I did not plan to write this book. I began to write a book that expanded on my earlier work on the concept of the sacred.[1] After years of teaching and consulting to organizations on improving the quality of work life and productivity, I have recently been pursuing my passion of the dialogue between religion, science, and spirituality.

I wanted to identify what the three domains of science, religion, and spirituality had in common and how they were different. My guiding question was, "Are there simple rules that each domain follows to determine what is real and true?" I began with the assumption that each domain needs only one way of knowing to present its truth.

I soon realized that all three domains need to draw upon multiple ways of knowing, although often there is a strong preference for only one way. But what are these ways of knowing?

Thus the idea for this book was born. My new guiding question was: "What are the multiple ways of knowing that are needed to fully understand reality and the truth claims in the various fields of knowledge?"

I do have an undergraduate degree in philosophy, so I knew something about the discipline called *epistemology*, the theory of the scope and nature of knowledge. But I did not have and could not find a practical model to describe and compare the multiple ways of knowing.

At this point I was discussing the science-religion dialogue with Dr. James Reho, my Episcopal-Lutheran pastor, and Dr. Charles (Billy) Gunnels, associate professor of biology at Florida Gulf Coast University. We wrestled with our understanding of epistemology and came up with the Ways of Knowing Model that is the basis of this book. I regret that their busy schedules kept them from continuing with the project. I hope our dialogue about religion, science, and spirituality using the Model will continue.

As I began to explicate the Model and apply it to issues, I was reminded of a dream I had on March 2011. The dream was:

> I am about to speak to a congregation. Someone tells me there is a priest who
> is afraid of me. I say that is to be expected. I see the pastor and go up the aisle
> to meet him. He is tall. He asks me, "What is the syntax for the session?" I tell
> him it is from both the Old and New Testaments. He says, "I thought it would
> be from the future."

---

1   This book on exploring the sacred was self-published (Olson, 2009) and only used in workshops I presented on the subject, mostly in churches.

Besides being the Ides of March, a day that foretold the future of Julius Caesar, the dream came at a time when my pastor, Walter Fohs (to whom this book is dedicated), and I were attending a Science for Ministry program at Princeton Theological Seminary. I was thinking about writing on the science and religion dialogue. Walter is tall and certainly a person I looked to for counsel. The warning that I would be raising fears with some members of the church establishment made sense to me given the "heretical" views that I was developing.

What puzzled me about the dream was the word *syntax*, not a word that I ordinarily think of or use. The Greek term from which syntax is derived means "joining of several things together."[2] In writing, it means the rules for making meaning by arranging words to form understandable phrases and sentences.

The challenge by the religious figure in the dream to take my syntax from the future rather than the Bible left me wondering. I was certainly not opposed to going beyond the stories and lessons of the Bible, but what is a future syntax? In analyzing the dream at that time I wrote down:

> I should be about using a syntax that is required for the twenty-first century.
> New rules are needed for what we see the future unfolding to be.

I was left wondering what are the rules of the new syntax?

As this book developed, one meaning of the dream became clear: creating a syntax, a structure, for understanding how fields of knowledge are evolving and connected using multiple ways of knowing. The rest of this book is an unfolding of the promise of my Ides of March dream.

---

2   http://grammar.about.com/od/rs/g/syntax.htm

Acknowledgments

I would like to acknowledge my friends and colleagues for their encouragement as I began this project. They include Arland Benson, Marilyn Bowman, Judy Charland, Rev. Charles Colberg, Mike Connelly, Dr. Peter Dickens, Mike Ducar, Dr. Bill Elliott, Tom Fisher, Rev. Walter Fohs, Ken Kostial, Dr. James Limburg, Rev. Bruce Sanguin, Vic Rinke, Rev. Paul Svingen, and Dr. Glenn Whitehouse.

I am grateful to Dr. James Reho, senior pastor at the Lamb of God Lutheran-Episcopal Church and Dr. Charles (Billy) Gunnels, associate professor and evolutionary biologist at Florida Gulf Coast University in Fort Myers who helped me with the epistemological issues in constructing the Ways of Knowing Model. Billy also designed the graphics of the Model.

Colleagues who provided helpful comments on the first draft of this book are Rev. Roger Brown, Judy Frye, Jody Ladwig, Rev. Cliff Lawrence, Bob Luther, Dr. Eric Olson, Rev. Bruce Sanguin, and Rev. Walter Schuman.

Persons providing valuable input on the final draft include Dr. Lynn Bondurant, Rev. Charles Colberg, Shane Hadden, Marion Howell, Ken Kostial, Dr. Kristine Quade, Rev. Becky Robbins-Penniman (whose many ideas I have incorporated into the text), Edward Wachter, and Mary Ann Whalen. Kassie Monsees obtained the pictures and Kathy Reasbeck helped with the references. The Archway Publication staff was very helpful in guiding me in the final phases.

Many thanks to Glenda Eoyang for writing the foreword and continuing to extend our collective knowledge of human system dynamics.

I am most grateful for the steadfast love and support from Judith through our over fifty years of marriage and for postponing some fun times together while I wrote this book.

Ed Olson
July, 2014

Introduction

WHY READ THIS BOOK?

Few people think about how they know things. The "obvious" is not always true. But how do we know? How do we find out the reality about what matters most to us? How do we know what actions to take?

Much of the time we are under great pressure to find simple answers to complex issues. We are asked to choose—Democrat or Republican, pro-life or pro-choice, union or right-to-work, etc. The way the issues are framed and the words and metaphors chosen on each side of the argument are designed to structure our reality (Dowd, 2008). Talk-radio show hosts often favor one way of thinking or acting without considering and often ridiculing any other possibilities.

We all have our preferred ways of knowing things. This is fine, unless we become locked into only one way to view reality. The truth that emerges from multiple ways of knowing helps us to be more resilient, see meaning in seemingly unrelated events, and gain a greater measure of certainty about our purpose. This serves not only our own interests but those of humanity and the planet as well.

This book is a guide for creative inquiry into perplexing problems and important issues. By accessing four ways of knowing, the reader can overcome one-sided thinking about knowing reality and what is the truth.

WHO SHOULD READ THIS BOOK?

The concepts, methods, and models in this book should be useful to four groups of potential readers.

1. Persons who want to expand their worldview will profit from a deeper understanding and application of the four ways of knowing.
2. Students and book discussion groups can use the Model to broaden their perspectives about the topics they are studying.
3. Teams, groups, and organizations faced with complex issues will find the Model a helpful problem-solving and decision-making tool for both unpacking their own thinking and discerning how others view the issues.
4. Anyone who wishes to explore hidden aspects of significant religious, philosophical, ethical, organization, and global issues.

How the Book is Organized

Self-Assessment: Readers are encouraged to complete the self-assessment at the end of this introduction as an approximate guide to their preferred ways of knowing before proceeding. Suggestions for interpreting the self-assessment are in chapter 3.

Chapter 1: *What* We Know. There are two dimensions of knowing: (1) our *perception* abilities of *intuition* and *sensing* and (2) our capacity to make *meaning* of what we have personally *experienced* or what has been *ascribed* by others. A story about mining for gold (an analogy to searching for reality) is used to illustrate how both dimensions, when combined, yield four ways (modes) of knowing.

Chapter 2: *How* We Know. The four ways (modes) of knowing are described using the Apollo 13 mission as an example. (1) *Insight* is the experienced meaning an individual has based on his or her intuition about reality. (2) External *authority* is the meaning that is ascribed by others based on their intuition of what is true and important. Over time we internalize much of this authority. (3) *Empiricism* is the meaning that is ascribed to what the senses detect about reality. (4) *Praxis* is experienced meaning based on what individuals have perceived by their own senses. The four modes each contribute a different aspect of our understanding of reality and our judgments about the truth of a situation.

Chapter 3: Avoiding One-sidedness. The use of all four modes helps us avoid the problem of being certain and self-righteous based on only one way of knowing. Exemplars and persons we admire likely draw upon all four ways of knowing. Specific steps are suggested to ensure a fruitful interactions of the modes.

Chapter 4: Creative Interaction. The interaction of all four of the ways of knowing leads to the emergence of new knowledge and surprising, novel, and transformative awareness in a process of creative emergence. The interaction during an improvisational theater performance and the parable of the Good Samaritan illustrate the point.

Chapter 5: Taking Adaptive Action. The Ways of Knowing Model helps to answer the questions necessary for taking action that is adaptive to present circumstances. A daily life example of developing a diet and exercise plan and a more esoteric topic of "what is the meaning of 'the sacred'" illustrate how the four ways of knowing amplify the questions of what is the situation, what is significant, and now what do I do?

Chapter 6: Finding Reality. Individuals can change core assumptions, reduce the power of dysfunctional archetypal patterns, and clarify their purpose by going deeper into the multiple ways of knowing. Societal issues such as moral leadership, religious organizations, and a global ethics can be explored with the Model. A case study illustrates how the Model can also be applied to practical organizational problems.

The chapters are best read in order because the new concepts are defined and examples are given when they first appear in the book. Questions for reflection and possible action steps for individuals and groups, based on the chapters' themes, are at the end of each chapter.

Self-Assessment

Purpose: To assess your preferred ways of knowing.

The reader is encouraged to complete this assessment before reading chapter 2 which explains the four ways of knowing that are measured by the self-assessment. In chapter 3 there are suggestions for how the assessment can be used.

Instructions: Allocate ten points among the four responses to each of the following ten situations. Give the most points to the response or responses you prefer. You may allocate the ten points in any way you like to indicate your preferences. For example, you may assign a "0" or "10" to a response.

Example: When I go for a walk or a ride, I:
  __2__ A enjoy the scenery.

  __3__ B like to go fast.

  __0__ C take a dog along.

  __5__ D like human company.

1. **When faced with a complex task, I will:**

  _____ A look at the big picture.

  _____ B look for expert advice.

  _____ C be sure I have the relevant facts.

  _____ D tackle what is "doable" first.

2. **Generally, I prefer to read a book that:**

  _____ A explores new horizons.

  _____ B has been written by a well-respected author.

  _____ C is based on accurate information.

  _____ D gives me something practical I can apply.

3. **In choosing a new beverage to drink in a restaurant, I would:**

  _____ A choose one that makes me curious.

  _____ B want to know what others have recommended.

  _____ C find out the main ingredients.

  _____ D sample the beverage, if possible.

4. **In choosing to continue with a medical doctor, I:**

_____ A go with my overall impression.

_____ B rely on the advice of others.

_____ C look for information about their education and certification.

_____ D need to experience how I am treated.

5. **In ordering food from a delicatessen, I would:**

_____ A imagine how it tastes.

_____ B choose what the server recommends.

_____ C want to know the major ingredients.

_____ D taste a sample, if available.

6. **Regarding the possibility of a divine presence, I consider:**

_____ A my intuition.

_____ B my religious tradition.

_____ C what has been proven to be true.

_____ D my experience.

7. **In assessing a political issue, I:**

_____ A trust my instincts.

_____ B want to know what the experts have to say.

_____ C want to know the relevant pros and cons.

_____ D like to have a personal experience with the issue.

8. **I base my decisions about finance on:**

_____ A my general sense of what is happening.

_____ B what financial advisors forecast.

_____ C the available evidence that I can gather.

_____ D my personal experience with the topic.

9. **If I were to coach a young person about choosing a career, I would:**

_____ A share my insights.

_____ B present some principles to guide them.

_____ C be sure my facts are correct.

_____ D encourage them to gain some first-hand experience.

10. **When faced with an ambiguous moral situation, I:**

_____ A usually have insight about what to do.

_____ B rely on my beliefs and values to decide what to do.

_____ C look for solid evidence about alternative courses of action.

_____ D like to test a course of action before I decide.

Add up the points you assigned to each response in situations 1-10 and record below:

A _____

B _____

C _____

D _____

Total ___100___

The instructions for interpreting the self-assessment are at the end of chapter 2.

CHAPTER 1

What We Know

To introduce *what* we know, let us start with a story about mining for gold. It is a good metaphor for both reality and effective action. The story was inspired by a program on the Discovery Channel.

SEARCHING FOR GOLD

Johnny asks his father and mother, "How do you find out if something is true?" His mother replies, "You have to search for it. It is like searching for gold. It takes considerable effort, but it is worth it in the end."

The parents proceed to tell the boy a story about gold mining in Alaska. Here is how the story went.

The Jones family had been gold miners in Alaska for years. They used big machinery to dig up dirt and rocks and process it to find flakes and small nuggets of gold (figure 1.1 shows a typical mining operation). Grandpa Jones was now over ninety and close to dying from cancer but had the intuition that there was a vein of gold in Big Creek, an area he had never explored. His dream was to see if that was true before he died. His family knew of his dream, and his young grandsons were determined to make his dream come true.

Figure 1.1: Mining for Gold

They knew that Grandpa might not live to see another gold mining season.

So, although winter was approaching and they had only a few days before everything froze and made digging impossible, the grandsons dug in the creek. After a week, at the last minute, they found gold nuggets.

Johnny asked, "So how is this like finding out whether something is true?"

His father said, "Well, Grandpa Jones had a dream that there was gold to be found in Big Creek. He wanted to see if that was true before he died. Grandpa's vision inspired his grandsons to try, even to venture out in terrible weather conditions, and dig to find gold. Of course, if Grandpa Jones had not told the grandsons how to dig for gold and that gold is often found near the bedrock of a creek, they would not have known how to start. They had specific information about the depth of the dirt on top of the old creek bed and they had the equipment they needed to dig."

Johnny said, "I still don't get it."

His mom pondered and wrote a list of four things:

Expert advice on where to mine for gold

A hunch and idea where gold might be

Specific information about the creek bed and the right kind of equipment

Willingness to take action

The father pointed to the list and said, "See, to find gold you need four things—a hunch, expertise, specific information and the right equipment, and the willingness to take risks. It is the same thing in trying to find out if anything is true. You have an intuition that guides you, you learn about what others know, you gather whatever facts and data you can, and you have to be willing to dig even though the payoff is uncertain."

Johnny said, "Now I think I get it. You can't find out if something is true by knowing just one thing. You have to use many kinds of knowledge to find the truth or, in this case, to find gold."

"Great," said his mother, "you have got it. By the way, although the goal was to find gold, Grandpa Jones and his family found something else."

"What was that?" Johnny asked.

His mom said, "They found great joy and a pride of accomplishment, but most of all they found out what united them as a family—the love they had for each other. That is the way it is when you use multiple ways of knowing things, the reality is you usually get much more than you expect."

THE TWO DIMENSIONS OF KNOWING

This story is a metaphor for the ways of knowing presented in this book and how using multiple ways of knowing pays off in finding out what is real, including something greater than ourselves. Finding the gold nuggets needed Grandpa's intuition and inspiration; the grandsons' motivation, energy, and action; the inherited knowledge of how to dig for gold; and the specific information about the creek and how to use the proper equipment. Using only one or two sources of knowledge would have led nowhere. I will use this story in the next chapter to illustrate the four ways of knowing. In this chapter I will describe the big picture. The question is, *what* do we know?

We know that (1) we *perceive* things (perception) and that (2) the things we perceive have *meaning* (meaning). These are the two basic dimensions of knowing. When they are combined, they create the four ways of knowing discussed in chapter 2.

PERCEPTION DIMENSION

The perception dimension is about what we notice and focus on. It is the mental act or process by which we acquire knowledge, including *sensing* (our five senses) and our *intuition*.

Everyone in the Jones family used their five senses and their intuition as they planned the project. They noticed and focused on Grandpa's hunch about finding gold. This is intuition—awareness of something beyond our senses– often called our "sixth sense." The family was also very aware of the material reality of the situation. They had a lot of charts, measurements, tests about the soil on top of the creek bed, and had the equipment to do the job. In their time planning together and talking about the project they used all of their five senses—sight, touch, smell, hearing, and taste.

The intuition and sensing aspects of perception are discussed below in more detail. If you are confident that you understand perception, you can skip to page 6 where the meaning dimension is discussed. However, a word of caution: our perception, whether by our senses or our intuition, can fool us. We perceive something one way, and then again … See figure 1.2.

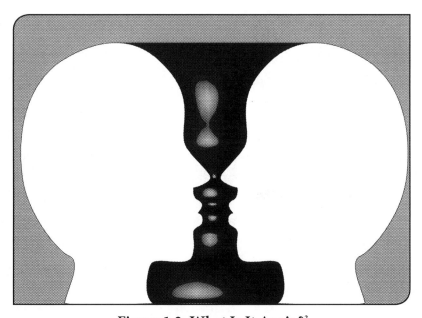

Figure 1.2: What Is It Again?[3]

---

3   Do you see two faces, a vase, or both?

INTUITION

Intuition is the reality that is not easily described in our tangible, material world. This is the realm of the unconscious, dreams, and flashes of insight. We feel and experience this reality, but to engage and describe it we need to go beyond our conventional means of analysis and description.

Intuition is a word with a lot of history. It can have two meanings.[4]

1. Intuition as a pre-understanding of something I may later come to understand and know theoretically—Newton first sees the apple fall and has a hunch that some "force" caused it to do so (intuition); then he works out the gravitational laws. Philosophers often mean this when they say intuition.
2. Intuition as knowledge of something "beyond" the empirical world and/or beyond thought categories, insight into "something more" that cannot in principle lead to theoretical knowledge later on because the reality it indicates is beyond words and/or sense experience. Common usage of the word intuition often means this.

I use both meanings in describing this aspect of Perception. Figure 1.3 suggests that we have a "third eye" to "see" that there is something beyond what we can verify with our senses. What we perceive through intuition can be uncertain, confusing, and mysterious, but as we become adept at using intuitive capacities, the new insights we gain can give us hope about what may happen in the future. Many have the intuition that an intelligent power is active in the world. Scientists regularly describe the mystery of the awesome wonder of the natural world, the presence of dark energy and dark matter in the universe, and the capacity of matter to self-organize.

Figure 1.3: Intuition

Barfield (1965) and Andrew Cohen (2011) equate intuition with the unmanifest dimension of reality, the unseen, unfathomable dimension. People experience intuition when they let go of thought, feeling, and time—a static and unchanging, beginningless and endless, timeless and formless dimension. The presence of intuition is so profound and pervasive that many people, going back to Meister Eckhart in the thirteenth century and more recently to Paul Tillich, say that ultimately God, the "ground of all being," can only be known through intuition.

---

4   I am grateful to Glenn Whitehouse for making these distinctions.

An extreme focus on intuition can lead to a kind of solipsism—a denial of objective evidence about the nature of reality.

Sensing

Sensing is what we discover through our five senses of taste, smell, touch, sight, and hearing (figure 1.4). As a species we use our senses and our reasoning ability to describe the principles, patterns, and dynamics that we observe. We use our senses to apprehend our human condition, our spiritual longings, the biosphere, the evolution of life, the scale of the universe, our development of religious traditions, and the dynamics of matter and energy. Using our senses and our instruments of analysis, we have identified tangible evidence to support our conclusions about all of these things, and achieved a high degree of predictability.

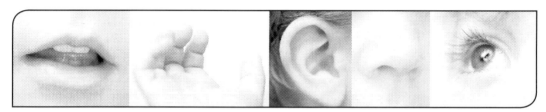

Figure 1.4: Sensing

If we place complete trust in our senses we are certain and clear about everything. We do not have doubt. Everything is black and white with no room for ambiguity. An extreme focus on perceived and objective phenomena leads to a reductionism that says everything can be explained by its material components.

Using Both Intuition and Sensing

Although our intuition and our senses are separate ways of perceiving things, we function best if the two ways work together. We can imagine something we desire, but we need to use our senses to attain it. Conversely, our senses perceive something, but without imagination we do not know what to do with it.

In their book on creating productive meetings, Dick and Emily Axelrod (2014) provide suggestions for integrating sensing and intuition. "Discovering the way things are" is vital in addressing important issues in meetings. This is sensing the current state of things. To go forward into the future they also argue that it is essential to "elicit people's dreams" — what they care about. This is using intuition.

For example, we collectively imagined and hoped for a peaceful and democratic Iraq before Saddam Hussein was deposed. The reality of the divisive sectarian differences in the society to the present day has revealed the difficulty of that vision. Not to imagine the possibility of a resolution of those differences leads to despair. The challenge is to embrace both realities—a hopeful future and the current realities. The reality of the Iraqi society is its pattern, history, and meaning to those who experience it. Engaging with such realities with an intuition that things could be better is the hope that can change reality.

Either of these aspects of perception can get us into trouble if we do not examine our assumptions. We can draw faulty conclusions based on either our intuition or senses. In the Iraq example, government policymakers concluded that our knowledge of the Iraqi culture and society was good enough to predict what would happen after the overthrow of Saddam. They were wrong. We also had the intuition that the spread of democracy was inevitable, not unlike the Manifest Destiny myth that is ingrained in U.S. culture. We were clearly wrong there as well.

> Personal example: I had strong intuitions about the ideas I wanted to include in this book, but I needed to draw upon my sensing abilities to write about the ideas in a way that readers would understand and appreciate.

How we understand all of the information from our senses and intuition is the subject of the next section (meaning).

MEANING DIMENSION

The previous section discussed the perception[5] dimension. It included sensing and intuition. As our intuition and senses interact with our logical thought processes, patterns begin to form that produce meaning.

The Jones family made meaning of the situation in two ways: (1) Their own personal experiences with mining (experienced meaning) suggested that Grandpa's vision and the data and equipment they had was sufficient for the task. (2) The expertise and written records of previous miners (ascribed meaning) about Big Creek was sufficient for them to go ahead.

Figure 1.5: Meaning Creates Coherence

As we developed as a species, meaning emerged from the material and social reality of the time period. From the cave paintings fifty thousand years ago to the abstract metaphors and drawings of scientists and artists today, we are the meaning makers (Weick, 1995; Frankl, 2006). The process of observing, naming, and theorizing that we do to make meaning amidst uncertainty is

---

5   Whereas the perception dimension corresponds to Jung's theory of perceiving, the meaning dimension does not correspond to Jung's judging dimension, which includes thinking and feeling, Jung's labels for the two ways we make decisions. The dimension of meaning in this book is derived from the work of Letiche, Lissack, and Schultz (2011). Jung's thinking and feeling functions are an aspect of every mode of knowing since we can make decisions on the basis of information independently in each mode.

itself meaningful. Sean Carroll, a theoretical physicist (in Brockman, 2012), says: "The world keeps happening, in accordance with its rules; it's up to us to make sense of it and give it a value" (p. 9).

Meaning puts pieces of the puzzle together (figure 1.5). Meaning gives us the confidence that we are on solid ground. The certainty it provides promotes our willingness to act. Meaning lets us create a story or rationale based on ideas and data we trust.

If you are confident that you understand the experienced and ascribed aspects of meaning you should proceed to chapter 2 where the two dimensions of perception and meaning are combined to yield the four ways of knowing.

EXPERIENCED MEANING

Experienced meaning is our own understanding of the world as we engage with life. It is direct, immediate, and related to the context we are in. Experienced meaning is about knowing one's self and our actions and taking responsibility. It is subjective, concrete, and existential. It forms our values, biases, intentions, and actions. We make meaning in an ongoing process of dialogue between ourselves and the situations we experience. These experiences may unsettle us, but they open our perceptions and help us make our way in the world. Experienced meaning was particularly important as women, persons of color, and the LGBT community found their voices and when friendships were formed across all categories of difference.

Figure 1.6 illustrates how we can experience meaning in multiple ways—in our minds, and bodies and from both internal and external stimulations. As we evolve, we can let go, at least temporarily, of what

Figure 1.6: Experienced Meaning

we believe (ascribed meaning) and find what is true about our beliefs and our reality from our experience. Extreme examples would be the culture shock of a child of Amish parents who leaves that environment to make it on his/her own in the big city, or the graduate who volunteers for the Peace Corps and experiences the challenges of an impoverished country.

Experienced meaning also has limits. Our individual experience is episodic, fleeting, and known only to us individually. Until we share this knowledge with others we are not able to make truth claims that go beyond our subjective reality world. We need others to help us as we confront intellectual challenges, make moral choices, and develop social interaction skills.

ASCRIBED MEANING

Ascribed meaning is our understanding of the world based on the ideas and beliefs given to us by others. This meaning is socially constructed, indirect, conceptual, retrospective, categorical, defined, labeled, and mediated (Letiche, Lissack, Schultz, 2011). We know it through rules, principles, generalizations, conclusions, and mental models.

We absorb this meaning from others who have developed explanations for how everything became the way it is, including the causes of everything. Parental conditioning provides our initial belief system regarding such things as race relations, religious beliefs, moral standards, etc. These messages stick with us through our lives, for good or for ill.

Figure 1.7: Ascribed Meaning

For example, many believe words from religious literature literally because that is the way they were taught or because the words are in a treasured book (figure 1.7).

We select among these explanations and descriptions to make meaning of things, even though the explanations may be partial or even destructive of other truths. Many beliefs, religious dogma, and some concepts in science are accepted simply because they made sense to others and were passed down to us. For example, undergraduate chemistry students are told that electron orbitals are of given shapes. Most of the students could not explain *why* these shapes are what they are; they just embrace it and go on. This is ascribed meaning. This is the basis of learning, tradition, and history, and essential to the development of human culture. Without it we would have to reinvent everything ourselves when we are born.

Thus, in many instances it makes good sense to rely on what we have learned from others. However, when we continue to limit reality only to what has already been ascribed, including from the internet and social media, we miss out on new learning.

Nietzsche said that "an excessive concern for the past would lead to a sickness." Although "some historical knowledge is advantageous and necessary for life, too much of it would be disadvantageous, having a harmful effect on the quality of our life itself" (Sinclair, 2004, p. 3).

Using Both Experienced and Ascribed Meaning[6]

Our experience and what we are told both contribute to *meaning*. To understand fully the entire scope of reality we need to attend carefully to both—to the knowledge and wisdom that has been passed down to us and also to the reality of our own subjective personal experience that can enrich knowledge that we have inherited from others.

An event might be known in different ways. For example, you might have an experience that is beyond ordinary consciousness and come away with direct experiential information that God is love; I might simply like an idea about God from a religious leader and choose to believe it is true. For you, then, this event is experienced meaning, but for me this knowledge is ascribed meaning. This example highlights the importance of the subject's engagement and relationship with what is being "known." A given object of knowledge can be experienced as both experienced and ascribed meaning.

The coherence of meaning—rigid or loose—needs attention. If our ascribed or experienced meaning has inconsistencies and does not hold up under scrutiny, it needs to be tightened. On the other hand, if our ascribed or experienced worldview is so tightly coherent that it automatically excludes anything that doesn't fit, it needs to be loosened. Some bumper stickers celebrate this position: "My mind is made up. Don't bother me with facts." Or "The Bible says it. I believe it. Period." If the beliefs we have inherited are held either too tightly or too loosely, they will not be able to withstand examination and inquiry. We will not be open to dialogue with different views or allow space for modifying our beliefs.

> Personal Example: As a college professor most of my life, I lived in a world where meaning was ascribed. I was either passing on the expert opinions of others or I was the expert telling others. As a process consultant in organizations, my role was to help people learn from their own experience rather than blindly following procedures or what worked in the past. In writing this book it was easiest to introduce and discuss the ideas of others (ascribed meaning). More challenging was drawing on my own experience and telling my own story (experienced meaning).

Summary

The dimension of perception provides information to us through our senses and our intuition.

Intuition was a major factor in forming the lives of early civilizations and it continues today as the frontiers of all of our academic disciplines push beyond the boundaries of what can be known with certainty. Our sensing capability is expanding at an exponential rate, aided

---

6   This discussion of meaning is about what we consciously do. We also experience unconscious coherence in our bodily processes. Our heart pumps and our blood circulates without the involvement of our conscious mind, although we can influence the rate at which these systems operate.

by what Kevin Kelly (2010) calls the "technium." Kelly describes the technium as the "rapid physical accumulation of the visible technology we have created and the organizations that form modern culture" (Figure 1.8).

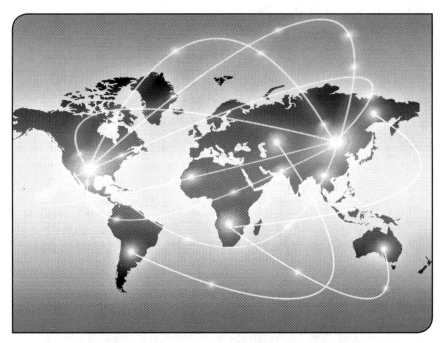

Figure 1.8 Interconnections of the Technium

The dimension of meaning makes coherent sense of the information from our senses and intuition. It does this as we have personal experience with that information (experienced meaning). We individually figure out meanings about our intuitions—dreams, premonitions, excitements—but we need to act to test any claims about truth for ourselves.

As we interact with others, with technology, and the collected written and symbolic knowledge in the world (ascribed meaning) we gain collective support for our intuitions from others who have experienced similar thoughts, ideas, or dreams. This gives us some confidence about what is true. Coupled with the rational methods and tests conducted by others, we are able to establish a high degree of certainty.

Questions for Reflection

Reflect on a recent big decision you have made.

1. We use either our senses or our intuition to perceive what is real and important. As you made the big decision, was your sense perception or your intuition more important, or both?

2. We make meaning on the basis of our experience or on what we learn from others. Which was more important in making the big decision, or were both important?

POSSIBLE ACTIONS

Ask for feedback from a trusted friend about:

1. Your use of your intuition compared to your use of your senses. Do you use both appropriately?

2. Whether you rely more on your experience or on what you have learned from others. Do you need to change?

C H A P T E R   2

How We Know

As discussed in chapter 1, through perception we receive information from our intuitions, from the senses, or from both. When combined with our capacity to experience or receive meaning, the two dimensions of what we know yield four ways or modes of knowing: insight, authority, empiricism, and praxis.

		MEANING	
		Ascribed	**Experienced**
PERCEPTION	**Intuition**	Authority	Insight
	Sensing	Empiricism	Praxis

In this chapter the four modes of knowing are explained with examples from the gold mining story and the story of the Apollo 13 mission.

APOLLO 13

What happened on the Apollo 13 mission to the moon in April, 1970, (figure 2.1) is well documented in interviews with the astronauts and NASA personnel, and the story is dramatically portrayed in the 1995 movie starring Tom Hanks and Bill Paxton.[7]

The commander was Jim Lovell; the pilot of the lunar module called the *Aquarius* was Fred Haise; and the pilot of the command module called the *Odyssey* was Jack Swigert.

On April 13 an oxygen tank exploded,

Figure 2.1

7   http://www.universetoday.com/63673/13-things-that-saved-apollo-13-part-10-duct-tape/#ixzz2w4TCtLUg. Retrieved June 26, 2014.

causing the moon landing to be aborted. Commander Lovell radioed NASA saying, "Houston, we've had a problem." That turned out to be a huge understatement because the crew had to abandon the *Odyssey* and use the *Aquarius* as a lifeboat to get back to earth.

Because the *Aquarius* was built only for two astronauts, carbon dioxide (CO_2) levels started getting dangerously high. The *Aquarius* had lithium hydroxide canisters to remove the CO_2 for two men for two days, but on board were three men trying to survive in this lifeboat for four days. However, with a little ingenuity and duct tape, the Houston team was able to let a totally unplanned but effective reconfiguration of the material emerge and, literally, make "a square peg fit in a round hole."

They splashed down safely and were soon on the deck of the recovery ship, the *USS Iwo Jima* on April 17, 1970. How they fixed the CO_2 problem is the dramatic story which provides examples of the four ways of knowing in action.

INSIGHT (EXPERIENCED MEANING THROUGH OUR OWN INTUITION)

When we experience meaning through our intuition, we have insights. This way of knowing includes our ability to pre-understand something we may later be able to know theoretically and our ability to sense "something more" that is beyond words and not able to be described by our senses. Insight includes both self-knowledge and knowledge of ultimate reality.

Insight as experienced by an individual is a mystical, wondrous, and awesome flash of understanding and epiphany. Einstein (in Frank, 1947) called this way of knowing an emotion, a feeling:

> The most beautiful emotion we can experience is the mystical. It is the power of all true art and science. He to whom this emotion is a stranger, who can no longer wonder and stand rapt in awe, is as good as dead. To know that what is impenetrable to us really exists, manifesting itself as the highest wisdom and the most radiant beauty, which our dull faculties can comprehend only in their most primitive forms—this knowledge, this feeling, is at the center of true religiousness. In this sense, and in this sense only, I belong to the rank of devoutly religious men.

From the earliest times, as our ancestors experienced mysterious phenomena, they intuited that there is "something more" beyond the phenomena themselves. They had experiences that were beyond words and concepts. The cave drawings of fifty thousand years ago suggest that humans were awed by the behavior of the animals they saw and attempted to capture their spirits on the cave walls. This original intuitive ability to imagine something more is still with us today—witness the modern media of movies, theater, television, literature, and art that create images to transform us.

We experience the something more in dreams, meditation, relationships, and in nature, as did Francis of Assisi. We listen for the emergence of the new and look for experiences of unity, creativity, the ecstatic, and the sacred.[8] This is the mode of empathy and awareness of things whole. In this mode we can find a unitive consciousness and inspiration.

> *Gold Mining Example*: Grandpa Jones experienced a strong insight that gold was on the river bed of Big Creek. He had a vision that he could not shake off, a vision strong enough to urge his grandsons to brave the elements to prove his dream to be correct.

> *Apollo Example*: There were plenty of filters in the *Odyssey*, but they were square and wouldn't fit in the *Aquarius* barrel. Woodfill said, "Without some kind of unusual miracle of making a square peg fit into a round hole the crew would not survive." Arabian said, "I need those guys to come up with an answer on the CO_2 thing and do it fast!" He was referring to the "tiger team" led by Ed Smylie, the crew systems manager working on the problem. The team had the insight that a "miracle" could be found.

The crew also needed a solution to hold the contraption together. Woodfill had this thought: "Use cardboard log book covers to support the plastic." It worked, but they had to figure out how the funnel could be fashioned to prevent leaking. Fortunately, the duct tape had been stowed onboard every mission since early in the *Gemini* days.

Figure 2.2

> *Personal Example*: I had a dream of driving my car in which the car went onto the shoulder of the road and I was fearful of driving into the ditch. I reflect over whether I was being careless and getting off track. When I awoke I thought of instances in my life when I need to be more careful.

Our insights can also induce disorder, uncertainty, and unpredictability. This mode is characterized by unconnected events, random

---

8   The terms *holy* and *sacred* are derived from *sacer*, the Roman word meaning "to be set apart." For the Romans *sacer* referred to the interior of a temple where people were expected to pay attention to a different quality of experience (Bell, 2013). The ancient Hebrews attributed these experiences to the *ruach* of God— the breath of God. Rudolph Otto (1917) called them the "Wholly Other," e.g., the experience of Moses with the burning bush. The sense of holiness as "other" goes back to the term *kadosh* in the Old Testament, which connected holiness with that which was other, or set apart.

activities, and surprises. We are not in control in this mode; if anything, we are controlled or seized by a muse, a spirit, the power of something beyond ourselves. A modern example is the ecstasies of Ramakrishna in which he would uncontrollably go into trance and ecstasy, sometimes for extended periods.

From a scientific perspective, the intuition of something more is an intellectual and aesthetic appreciation of the same object at the same time. Flashes of understanding, epiphanies and ecstatic experiences result in a profound altered state of consciousness. Many people may have the same insight, but individuals internalize the insight in their own particular ways. Moreover, as William James wrote in 1902, the revelations of the mystic hold true only for the mystic. Others may value the ideas, but they cannot make truth claims without having a similar experience. The light bulb in figure 2.2 is a frequent symbol in our culture for awakening to something new. It suggests that our insights are flashes of understanding that are particular to each individual.

Cox (2009) believes that the mixture of wonder and fear we experience toward the mystery that surrounds us is the beginning of faith. Whatever the something more is, we experience a life force that jolts us into the affirmation that whatever this is, it matters— it's serious. When we experience some meaning in that mystery, the awe becomes faith. If a person experiences a lack of meaning, they may have a crisis about their faith (Bell, 2013).

AUTHORITY (ASCRIBED MEANING THROUGH INTUITION)

When meaning based on the intuition of another or a group is given to us, we have *authority* as a way of knowing.

In the quest to understand the unknowns, humans intuited theories to explain the mysterious phenomena they experienced in places, objects, persons, rituals, times, and stories. This is the mode of participating in the unknown by interpreting and giving meaning to facts (hermeneutics). It is a collective discernment. It is the development of normative conventional wisdom, common belief, ethics, and morality.

Plato, Aristotle, tribal communities, churches, and nations have constructed theories and dogmas about the unknown to give security and certainty to their followers. In our societies and organizations we regularly subscribe to hierarchies and power structures that represent what we believe to be true and that are operating in our best interests (such as our Constitution represented in figure 2.3). Authority can provide an appropriate context for understanding the insights we have.

Figure 2.3: Authority

We believe our parents, teachers, prophets, and leaders who have ascribed meaning to the phenomena they experienced. We appropriate these propositions and develop a set of beliefs and develop practices that we hope will bring about better mental health and happiness. These beliefs and assumptions are necessary guides as we make decisions and go about our daily lives. For many, they form a pattern called a faith that provides a general sense of direction.[9] Religious, political, or social beliefs can lead people to work for peace, love, justice, and charity. But they can also lead to hatred, inequity, and war.

These beliefs have organized around and relied on commonly accepted external authorities. They may be common codes (scriptures, laws) or people. In more recent times there has been a shift to organizing around and relying on *internal* authority.

The shift to reliance on internal authority also helps to explain the fragmentation of knowledge in our society. Using internal authority may make the development of an autocratic central authority less likely, but it does have its downside in the loss of a widely-accepted sense of the public interest.

Gold Mining Example: The entire Jones family had accumulated wisdom and knowledge of how to mine for gold.

Apollo 13 Example: "Any of us in the Mission Evaluation Room (MER) might be called upon to assist in an Apollo 13 'solution,'" said Jerry Woodfill, who helped design and monitor the Apollo caution and warning systems. The MER

---

9   Wolpert & Tickle (2010) argue that human beliefs "originate from our unique ability to conceptualize that physical effects have physical causes. Once our ancestors had a concept of cause and effect they began to wonder about the causes of things that affected their lives, such as illness, death, pain, bad weather, hostile animals, and dreams." They believed there must be invisible agents in the external world—gods that cause these things.

was where the spacecraft systems engineers were stationed during a mission, and should a problem arise on any Apollo mission, the "MER-men," led by Don Arabian, were called on for expert advice.

Personal example: I attended a lecture and listened to an expert on Shakespeare. I assessed the credibility of the expert and compared what I heard to what I'd already learned about Shakespeare in college and decided if the information was consistent. I'd developed my own internal authority about Shakespeare.

Faith—in anything—is necessary. William James said that to most people faith means having faith in someone else's faith—a belief received second-hand from other believers (Hoeller, 2002). Hoeller says that, "A certain kind of faith (*pistis*) is faith in one's experience, a faithfulness that one feels toward one's experience of inner, liberating knowledge" (p. 13).

Scientists have faith in their methods. Physicists have faith that the laws of physics will not suddenly change tomorrow. They have faith the science that has worked for centuries will continue to work tomorrow. They hypothesize things they cannot yet explain. They predict things they have not yet directly observed but which fit with the current best model. Science has faith that there is ever more to discover and learn despite having never observed it.

EMPIRICISM (ASCRIBED MEANING THROUGH THE SENSES)

Empiricism is the way of knowing that combines perceiving reality with the five senses and the meaning that is ascribed to that reality. Empiricism separates instances of knowledge determined by the senses from instances of knowledge based on intuition or belief. Avery (2011) points out that the rigors of the experimental method turn individual perceptions into facts that all of us can believe.

People use the five senses to understand the material world that can be seen, touched, smelled, heard, and felt. The data from the senses and the theories and hypotheses that have been ascribed by others are used to explain the material universe. The mode is governed by procedures, rules, and policies of how knowledge is attained. It is highly predictable and constrained. The ruler in figure 2.4 suggests the effort involved in being certain about this knowledge. "Measure twice, cut once," is an axiom in carpentry.

Gold Mining Example: The team had specific measurements of the top soil and the physical equipment needed for the task.

Figure 2.4: Empiricism

Apollo 13 Example: Woodfill had worked with the environmental system engineers to establish an alarm level based on the percentage of CO_2 in the cabin atmosphere. He and Arabian carefully studied the data based on the known cabin pressure, the voltage output from the CO_2 transducer, and the voltage level at which warning electronics initiated the alarm.

At a mission debriefing, Jack Swigert noted, "At this point in time I think the partial pressure of CO_2 was reading about fifteen millimeters. We constructed two of these things and I think within an hour was down to two-tenths." Woodfill watched his systems from the MER. "I saw the alarm light go out and it stayed out the rest of the mission."

Personal Example: I read a scientific article that said researchers have found that individual fish in a school of fish decide to go in the general direction of the school rather than paying attention to what the neighboring fish are doing, as had been hypothesized. I believed it because the research team described their methods and made appropriate conclusions based on their data.

We cannot see or touch gravity, but it is one of the laws of this domain that can be tested and predicted. The many scientific disciplines have developed to systematically measure and describe this way of knowing. Science formulates hypotheses that can explain the evidence yielded from the tools it uses to measure and quantify reality. As science progresses, it continually defines and refines what it can actually measure that will fit these hypotheses or lead to the creation of new hypotheses. Any given hypothesis may not be the ultimate truth, but it serves as a useful approximation to the truth we need to understand and predict what happens in our world. The hypotheses and measurements are good enough to send a rocket to and from the moon, though we know there may be forces affecting that rocket that we do not understand, like dark energy and dark matter.

Some would posit that the objectivism of the empirical mode is the only way to discern "reality." Even with empiricism, however, we see the world through the lens provided by ascribed authority, not as the world "is." The filters and biases we have inherited influence our senses and can even limit what we are able to perceive.

Scientists use paradigms and models of how things work that are grounded in their own particular ways of knowing. These models have changed over the centuries as anomalies that do not fit the models are discovered. The fact that empiricism is affected by how we perceive things is clear from examples such as the Copernican revolution in astronomy, the Darwinian theory of evolution, and the quantum revolution in physics, which have not been easily accepted even within the scientific communities.

PRAXIS (EXPERIENCED MEANING THROUGH OUR OWN SENSES)

Praxis is the way of knowing that combines our perception of reality with our senses and ability to make meaning of that reality through our personal experiences. Praxis includes the feelings that accompany our senses (e.g. passion) and our will to take action. Unlike empiricism, which structures consciousness about the material world but does not know consciousness, praxis knows what consciousness is from the inside (Avery, 2011). Empiricism can tell us many things about water—its appearance, its weight, etc., but to really know water we need to drink it.

Figure 2.5: Praxis

Praxis is our experience of knowing through acting on our understanding and inner perceptions of who and how we are and why we are here. In praxis we attribute meaning to the information received through our senses. It is the process by which an idea, theory, lesson, or skill is enacted, practiced, embodied, or realized. Aristotle held that praxis was practical wisdom, a basic activity of humans to which end was practical knowledge and action.

In this way of knowing, something is true if it works. We engage in trials and learn by our successes or errors. We make things happen, or, with awareness, we allow things to happen.

Praxis is used by educators to describe the cyclical process of experiential learning. Praxis is doing something and afterward finding out it works as feedback loops inform us about the impact of the action. The concept of proprioception helps explain this learning-by-doing. It is how our fingers might remember something we played on a piano long ago even though our logical minds cannot. Figure 2.5 shows a man embracing what he can learn by actively experiencing nature.

Praxis is also important in meditation and spirituality wherein emphasis is placed on gaining firsthand experience of the divine, since the mind and our language are not able to comprehend or express the infinite. Matthew Fox (1988) explained it this way:

> Wisdom is always taste—in both Latin and Hebrew, the word for wisdom comes from the word for taste—so it's something to taste, not something to theorize about. "Taste and see that God is good," the psalm says; and that's wisdom: tasting life. No one can do it for us. It is about tasting and trusting experience before institution or dogma (p. 26).

Gold Mining Example: The grandsons were willing to try, to take risks and take action.

Apollo 13 Example: Using only the type of equipment and tools the crew had on board –including plastic Moon rock bags, cardboard, suit hoses, and duct tape — Smylie and his team conceived a configuration that might work. The contraption that Smylie and his team came up with was checked out in their simulators. It worked. The team quickly radioed instructions to the Apollo crew, carefully leading them through about an hour's worth of steps.

Personal Example: I attended a meditation workshop where I learned and developed new breathing techniques. It profoundly increased my sense of relaxation.

The concept of "taste" described by Fox can be amplified by "tasting" the activities of, for example, cooking and dance. Brady (2011) has developed a method of research called "cooking as inquiry" that recognizes the body and food-making as sites of knowledge. For example, when a person prepares food for a child, the child learns that the role of the cook in the family system is one of nurturer and helper. The child also learns which foods are considered desirable and tasty within their ethnic identity and culture. Snowber (2012) has also discussed dance as "a way for adults to be opened up to embodied learning to connect themselves with their bodies, mind, heart, and imagination and to more deeply understand and question the world around us" (p. 55).

Our actions and decisions in praxis move us to influence the patterns we see emerging at all levels where we live, work, and play. Bell (2013) says that the deep place within us where our desires reside is our *splagchnon* (bowels, guts)—the part of us from which we truly live. That seat of our being drives us to move, speak, act, touch, and feel. The man in figure 2.4 suggests that there is no option but to engage with the external world. We may fail, but our unconscious is at work in us, calling up all kinds of resolve, fiber and spine—what we need to face, know, name, and embrace in our environment. These interactions contribute to the continuous generation of meaning. Bell says that the energy in the universe flows through us; we are expressions of the sacred.

COMPARISON OF THE FOUR MODES

In table 2.1 the four modes are compared based on how information is received through perception, how it is processed and created through meaning, and how the mode contributes to a testing for truth.[10]

---

10   Eoyang and Holladay (2013) identify three kinds of truth: subjective, normative, and objective. They argue that a fourth kind of truth is "complex" truth, which acknowledges that the other three kinds of truth are equally valid depending on differing times and circumstances.

Table 2.1: Comparison of the Four Modes

Mode	What is Received (Perceiving)	How it is Processed (Meaning)	Test of Truthfulness
Insight	Intuitive, even mystical experiences	Our psyche makes sense of the experiences	Subjective; It is true for me.
Authority	What others have taught us based on their beliefs	We accept or reject what has been ascribed	Normative; It is true for those people or sources I respect.
Empiricism	External sensory data	Rational reflection based on what we have learned from others' sensory data	Objective; I or others can repeatedly measure it and get the same result.
Praxis	Kinesthetic, sensory experience of our body	Reflect on our felt experience and build new neural pathways in our brain	Pragmatic; I or others can make it work.

Insight helps us to *subjectively* decide whether something is "true for me and others."

Authority helps us to assess whether something is true for others and sources whom we respect. This is *normative* truth.

Empiricism provides *objective* measures to ascertain that something is true consistently or with a known variation.

Praxis uses our felt experience to assess if something is *pragmatic*, if it will work.

All of the theories of personality, decision-making, and epistemology use logic, analytic reasoning, and reflective rationality in determining how we know things and make decisions. In the four ways of knowing, these capacities are used in determining the truth claims and arguments. For example, we use reason to process knowledge from all four ways of knowing. When we intuit something we ask ourselves, "Does this make sense; is it logical?" When some authority tells us something is true, we ask ourselves, "Is this consistent with what I already know and believe?" When we are determining the facts of a situation we follow logical procedures of induction and deduction. When we are acting in the world, we continuously ask ourselves, "Does this make sense to do this now?"

SUMMARY

The four ways of knowing are unique and can individually help us succeed in life, but as we explore in the next chapter, the interaction of one mode with another is essential for dealing with the subtleties and complexities of living in a material world.

As depicted in the Apollo 13 movie, the Houston MER team (authority), an impressive array of engineers, was gathered around a table loaded with material that was also available on the spacecraft. They had all of the data about what was happening and would happen to the astronauts (empiricism). They had a hunch (insight) that they could accomplish the miracle of "making a square peg fit into a round hole" by using the square space suit filters, the log book covers to support the plastic, and duct tape to prevent leaking. The Houston team checked out (praxis) the "contraption" in the simulation and the instructions were relayed to the spacecraft.

Woodfill said, "The concept seemed to evolve as all looked on." This was a self-organizing process—the four modes interacted to produce a "miracle." The expertise, data, vision, and testing all worked together and the crew of Apollo 13 was saved. As Jim Lovell wrote in his book *Lost Moon* (Kluger & Lovell, 1994), "The contraption wasn't very handsome, but it worked."

QUESTIONS FOR REFLECTION

1. How is "insight" important in your life? Does it help or hinder you in your pursuit of the truth? Do you have an example of using insight to sense something more?

2. How is authority both a blessing and a curse? Where do you find it essential for your life, and where does authority limit your access to truth?

3. In what aspect of your life is empiricism most important? What are the limits to what you can know with your five senses?

4. In what aspects of life is it important to use praxis to know? What are examples of where praxis extended or deepened your knowledge?

POSSIBLE ACTIONS

1. Carry a journal with you at all times to record your insights. Record your dreams and look for insights that your unconscious is giving to your conscious mind.

2. Write a list of your most important beliefs. Reflect on which way(s) of knowing is the basis of those beliefs.

3. Choose a current topic of interest. Using a library, social media, or the internet, determine what is empirically and objectively known about the topic compared to beliefs and opinions.

4. Take a leisurely walk in nature and experience as much of it as you can by smelling, touching, listening, seeing, and (if you dare) tasting. Note the impact of this on your spirit.

Interpreting the Self-Assessment:

Copy your scores for the responses to A, B, C, and D and post in column A. In column B subtract your lowest score from your highest score.

Mode	Column A Score Total	Column B Score Differences	Notes:
A Insight		Highest Score _____	
B Authority		--Lowest Score _____	
C Empirical		Difference _____	
D Praxis			

Total 100

Your preferred way(s) of knowing are your high scores. The lowest score(s) suggest you use that mode(s) least.

If the scores among all four modes are roughly equal, you may not have a preferred way of knowing.

Re-reading the description of the four modes in this chapter will help you to determine if the self-assessment accurately identified your preferences.

Differences of eight or more points between the scores are likely to be significant. Differences of fifteen or more indicate that one of your high-scoring mode(s) may be a dominant mode(s) and another may be a "shadow" mode that is less used. Any pattern can be appropriate depending on your work, life style, or stage of life.

The question is, do you wish to use one or more modes more often and some modes less often in your own search for reality?

Chapter 3 contains additional suggestions for further analysis of your scores.

CHAPTER 3
Avoiding One-sidedness

Sometimes our preferences, training, or cultural backgrounds can limit our full use of the four modes of knowing and we can become one-sided. It is sometimes necessary to loosen or tighten the constraints our backgrounds have placed on one or more of the modes. In this chapter specific suggestions for adjusting those constraints are provided.

CONSTRAINTS

Any mode of knowing can be *under-constrained* or *over-constrained* and be required to deal with too much, too quickly, in too many places. In these instances we can seem out of control and unable to respond. In either case, if we can understand the impact some of the modes have on other modes we can find the means to change the level of constraint.

Under-constrained

When under-constrained we are unable to deal with the speed, diversity, and sheer volume of information that comes along. For example, when our insights run wild, we have so many ideas and scenarios in our minds that we can be paralyzed. We can overdo our quest for authority in our research, reading, and talking with experts until we have so much conflicting information that we do not know what to do. We may collect empirical data and make so many observations that we lose track of any patterns to the information. We can be so venturesome and try so many possible solutions to a problem (praxis) that we never actually accomplish anything.

Over-constrained

On the other hand, sometimes a way of knowing is over-constrained, limited in its ability to respond. In these instances we can be too controlled, too resistant to change, or too rigid. For example, we have an idea or vision (insight) which is so compelling that we cannot let it go. We have a strong belief system (authority) and do not wish to even hear any contradictions. We collect empirical information—or facts—which we believe cannot be set aside by other information that is available. We are fearful of trying new things (praxis) and confine our activity to what is tried and true for us. Our worldview can be so constraining that we do not see the impact we have on others.

In any learning situation there are aspects that need to be constrained and controlled to ensure the learning is understood and integrated. There are also situations where we need to be free to go wherever any of the modes of knowing want to take us.

To find reality our modes of knowing require a proper amount of constraint—not too much and not too little. In the following pages are some tips for adjusting the constraints on how we hold or bind the modes.

ANALYSIS OF MODE PREFERENCES

Before continuing to read about how to affect the constraints on the modes of knowing, the reader is encouraged to review the results of the self-assessment (chapter 2) and identify your favorite and least favorite ways of knowing. There are several possible patterns:

1. One dominant score. Are you very constrained and locked into that mode? If so, consider how you can loosen some of the ways you express that mode and risk opening to some of the other modes. It is likely that one of the other modes is far less used.

    For example, "Mira" had a high authority score. She was very tightly bound to what she had learned growing up. Her challenge was to let go of some of the doctrines that were not life-giving and trust her own insights, embrace the reality revealed by empirical evidence, and value her life experiences.

    "Jacob" had a high praxis score. As an artist he savored engaging with life and expressing his experience through his art. His lowest score was authority. He regularly found himself challenging conventional wisdom. To reduce some of the stress in his life, he needed to find sources of support in which he could believe. "Alice," a musician, also had a high praxis score. She knew how to play the notes expertly, but could not vary tonality when necessary in various venues. Her lowest score was empiricism. She needed to review research on acoustics.

2. All scores are approximately equal. If your scores are fairly evenly distributed over the four modes, you may be using all modes equally in your daily life. The challenge is to maintain an appropriate balance of constraint in your use of the modes, or perhaps experiment with greater use of one of the modes.

    "Ruth's" scores were about the same, but as she explored the value of each way of knowing she was determined to try new things (praxis) by traveling more and joining several book discussion groups.

3. Two higher scores. If you have two higher scores, it may be that your life is most meaningful for you when you rely on one of the two dimensions of knowing – ascribed meaning or experienced meaning.

"Judy's" two highest scores were insight and praxis. Things were most meaningful for her if she experienced them through her own intuition and senses (experienced meaning). She is a free spirit who primarily enjoyed life through quiet reflection and active practice of her values. She profited by learning to value external authorities, listening more to what experts and new research could teach her (ascribed meaning).

"Marco" had two high scores—authority and empiricism. Things were most meaningful for Marco if he knew that others vouched for them by their own beliefs or empirical data (ascribed meaning). He needed to learn to trust his own ideas and experience and take more initiative in experimenting with aspects of living that were not part of his daily routine (experienced meaning).

The next section provides examples of persons who have successfully drawn upon all four ways of knowing in their lives.

EXEMPLARS' USE OF THE FOUR WAYS OF KNOWING

To provide examples of persons who have generally balanced the constraints they placed on each mode, it is useful to look at the life of exemplars. You can identify a person (historical or living) who has influenced your life. To illustrate, I will list Plato, Jesus of Nazareth, Mohandas Gandhi, Eleanor Roosevelt, Ronald Reagan, and Bill Gates. All of these historical figures and exemplary contemporary leaders use all four ways of knowing with appropriate levels of constraint.

Plato

Insight: Wrote about the ideals of justice, courage, wisdom, and moderation of the individual and society.

Authority: Was taught the doctrines of Pythagoras and Parmenides that provided the foundation for his study of metaphysics and epistemology.

Empiricism: He studied geometry, geology, and astronomy in Egypt.

Praxis: Served in the Peloponnesian War and participated in politics. In later life he explored art, dance, music, and drama.

Jesus

Insight: Had many visions and revelations such as the voice of the Father at his baptism.

Authority: Demonstrated knowledge of the Jewish Torah in communications with his followers.

Empiricism: Within the limits of the scientific knowledge of the age, he was very aware of nature and the realities of life as demonstrated in his parables.

Praxis: Regularly astounded his followers by venturing where others feared to tread—visiting lepers and other outcasts, healing the sick, and confronting religious leaders.

Gandhi

Insight: Had visions about unifying all the peoples of India.

Authority: Knew the legal code of England and the wisdom of the East.

Empiricism: Saw the realities of colonialism on the life and culture of his people.

Praxis: In his acts of passive resistance and constructive nonviolence he demonstrated the power of Jesus's ethical teachings.

Eleanor Roosevelt

Insight: From an upbringing of a life of privilege, as First Lady she began seeing the deeper issues of human rights, children's causes, and women's status.

Authority: Was influenced by a noted feminist educator, Marie Souvestre; the idealist reformer, President Theodore Roosevelt (her uncle); and the social egalitarian founder of the Settlement House Movement.

Empiricism: Visited and listened carefully to coal miners in their dark mines, army soldiers in their muddy camps, and African-Americans in their ghettos.

Praxis: Authored the UN Universal Declaration of Human Rights, resigned from the DAR when it snubbed Marian Anderson, and wrote numerous newspaper columns and even disagreed publically with her husband's presidential policies.

Ronald Reagan

Insight: Had a vision of America as "a beacon of hope for those who do not have freedom."

Authority: The faith-based optimism in the goodness of people from his mother; the anti-communism policies of J. Edgar Hoover; and the conservative policies of executives of the General Electric company for which he was hired as a spokesperson.

Empiricism: Was very aware of the lack of personal freedom in communist countries and the economic success of capitalists.

Praxis: His decision to enter state and national politics was entirely based on his desire to effectuate his values, which in turn had global impact. A famous case in point is his statement: "Mr. Gorbachev, tear down this wall."

Bill Gates

Insight: Was fascinated with the possibilities that a personal computer could be a tool to feed our curiosity and inventiveness and empower us to use our creativity and intelligence to make the world a better place.

Authority: In early years in computer development his authorities were software programming language and engineering concepts and the freedom Americans have to be creative and innovative. The teachings of the Roman Catholic Church on the need to reduce inequality have shaped his later years.

Empiricism: Early on Gates noted that most systems (software, engineering, and management) could be improved by finding the weak spots, or "bugs," and fixing them. Later, he took note of problems affecting millions of poor people around the world.

Praxis: In the early days of his company he personally reviewed every line of code the company shipped, often rewriting the code as necessary. When analyzing any corporate move he would develop a profile of all the possible scenarios and run through them, asking questions about anything that could possibly happen. He later left Microsoft and set up the Gates Foundation to eliminate polio.

The next section discusses how each mode can impact the others and how you can loosen the constraints on modes that are underused and tighten the constraints on modes that are overused.

Interaction of the Four Modes

All four modes of knowing are representative of reality and truth, albeit from different sources. Insight represents subjective reality and the truth of individuals. Authority represents normative reality and the truths of a collective of people. Empiricism represents objective reality and truth as verified by evidence. Praxis represents the truth of our integrity as we act on our values, stated or unstated. All four modes are valuable and necessary for life. Their interaction and how they constrain each other can either dampen inquiry or lead to deeper levels of knowledge.

As two modes interact: (1) one mode can support and reinforce the learning and truth of the other mode; (2) one mode can suppress or cancel out what the other mode is offering; or (3) they can synergistically learn from each other and create new learning. For example, if I have an idea (insight) to buy a flat screen TV, I can solicit the opinions of my friends (authority). I can study the pros and cons of models featured in Consumer Reports (empirical). I can go to a local TV store and test the various models and sizes in action (praxis).

Similarly I could start with my friends' statements about how much they like their new televisions (authority), then check my own gut feeling about whether this is something I need (insight) and go to the other two modes as in the previous example. In this example, I might have started with reading *Consumer Reports*, or seeing a TV display when I went to a Best Buy store.

Taking one mode at a time, I will discuss how it can support, reinforce, or positively change the information and meaning in the other modes and how it can act as a negative constraint or even destructive force on the outcomes of the other modes.

The discussion of each mode will begin with an example of how it was used by the Jones family to find gold.

Insight

Without Grandpa Jones's insight, his dreams, and his strong hunch that gold nuggets were in the bedrock of Big Creek, the quest would not have begun.

Impact of Insight on Authority: Insight is essential for initiating change. If we check our ideas with our bosses they may be squelched (authority cancels insight), but they can also be praised and lead to positive change (insight improves authority). The decision to engage our insights with conventional wisdom will inevitably involve risk, misunderstandings, ridicule, or worse. But an individual's profound insight can also be positive, creative, and transformative for a community.

The beliefs we have inherited are sometimes not relevant for our present circumstances. The truth of the intuitions we experience can influence and even displace the intuitions of the past.

Impact of Insight on Empiricism: Einstein (1931) said:

> I believe in intuition and inspiration … At times I feel certain I am right while
> not knowing the reason. When the eclipse of 1919 confirmed my intuition,

I was not in the least surprised. In fact I would have been astonished had it turned out otherwise. Imagination is more important than knowledge. For knowledge is limited, whereas imagination embraces the entire world, stimulating progress, giving birth to evolution. It is, strictly speaking, a real factor in scientific research.

This is a powerful statement of the primacy of insight over empiricism by a preeminent scientist. The comprehensive view, the inclusiveness of insight that sees things whole, is not achievable by an empiricism that is reductive.

Insight from meditation, reflection, and dreams are revelations that provide purpose and direction. Imagination and insight give value and direction to empirical work. They tell us what to look for.

Barfield, writing in 1965, argued that both artists and scientists need to be creative and systematic in using imagination and intuition to increase our knowledge and to save us from viewing the world as a place of chaos and "inanity."

Impact of Insight on Praxis: To have value, a person's insights must be acted upon. The risk is that when translated into action, the awesome ideas become simplified and watered down and lose their luster and excitement. For example, when put into practice, detailed, rich dreams are usually only a shadow of what the dreamer experienced. Yet, not to take action would deny the power and truth of the insight. To be authentic and coherent, we must act on our great ideas.

Insights give us flexibility and instant adaptability when we take action. In the process of testing our hunches, insight helps identify our emotions, thoughts, sensations, attitudes, and our "gut" reactions.

When we speak from the truth of our insights, what belongs to us uniquely at the present moment, we change our direction—the steps we take in the world.

Reflection on the Power of Insight: The power of the truth and wholeness of insight is evident in these examples. It can trump external authority, enlighten empirical facts, and guide our action. Insight is our guiding light. It needs to be balanced with the wisdom in our culture, the objective reality, and our lived experience, but as in finding gold, it is essential to get us started.

Our flashes of insight are inherently mysterious. An ordinary moment suddenly means more, producing a sense of awe and wonder. There are many gateways to insights that are unpredictable, random, surprising, insightful, shocking, and challenging. Our challenge is to adjust the constraints on these insights so they can inform our beliefs, our empirical understanding of things, and the practical actions we take.

Tips for *loosening* constraints on insights:

- To engage empiricism, expose yourself to different cultures.

- To engage praxis, participate in events you usually do not go to with persons younger or older than you.
- To engage authority, browse the public library; take courses; attend lectures.
- In general, let your mind wander, pay attention to your dreams.
- In general, try aroma therapy, meditation, yoga, tai chi, or other physical activities that stimulate the right brain.
- In general, listen to music that will engage your emotions.

Tips for *tightening* constraints on insights:

- To engage the empiric, learn more about the culture you are in.
- To engage praxis, participate in events of your peer group.
- To engage authority, find experts you can respect; study what they have to say.
- In general, focus on one idea you are passionate about.
- In general, reduce the stimulation present in your environment.
- In general, find a type of music that is calming for you.

AUTHORITY

Grandpa Jones had an interesting idea, but without the knowhow about gold mining he had learned and passed on to his grandsons, they would have had to sit around the kitchen table and figure out how to search completely from scratch.

Impact of Authority on Insight: Our history, our culture, our strong beliefs about matters that are important to us—family, religion, politics, the economy, etc.—all contribute to a personal worldview that provides guides for our behavior and interactions with others. It is difficult for insights to emerge that contradict that legacy. To risk confronting those traditions requires great courage—the stuff of historic figures like Martin Luther, Abraham Lincoln, and Martin Luther King, Jr.

Impact of Authority on Empiricism: There are many contemporary examples of where authority suppresses empiricism, e.g., the continuing struggle to have people accept the facts of evolution and the 13.8 billion-year journey of the cosmos. Galileo's new telescope technology got him into trouble with church authority. During the Civil War, the scientist Semmelweis (1861) had the empirical evidence to propose that microbes are disease vectors, but the authorities wanted to put him in an insane asylum for insisting that surgeons should wash their hands.

There are many positive examples of authority guiding empirical research by proposing theories and hypotheses that are now able to be tested with new technology. The wisdom of our history and culture can provide guidance for how we construct our lives to face modern problems.

Impact of Authority on Praxis: The wisdom, morals, and ethics contained in our inherited legacy of Scripture, wise sayings, and exemplars are continually tested in order to adapt to the realities of the practical here and now.

There are principles and moral codes of authority that continue to influence ethical action, including the commandments, stories, and parables in the Bible (figure 3.1). For example, the prophet Nathan said to King David:

> There were two men in the same city—one rich, the other poor. The rich man had huge flocks of sheep, herds of cattle. The poor man had nothing but one little female lamb, which he had bought and raised. It grew up with him and his children as a member of the family. It ate off his plate and drank from his cup and slept on his bed. It was like a daughter to him. One day a traveler dropped in on the rich man. He was too stingy to take an animal from his own herds or flocks to make a meal for his visitor, so he took the poor man's lamb and prepared a meal to set before his guest.
>
> David exploded in anger. "As surely as God lives," he said to Nathan, "the man who did this ought to be lynched! He must repay for the lamb four times over for his crime and his stinginess!" "You're the man!" said Nathan.
>
> 2 Samuel 12:1–7 from *The Message* by Eugene Peterson

Figure 3.1: The Prophet Nathan and King David

The story is very relevant today.

Reflection on the Power of Authority: Authority can be a positive or constraining force on the other modes. The challenge is to respect and learn from the wisdom in authority while discovering when we need to break free from its grip.

As we seek to understand our experiences, meaning is attributed to them by our culture, our respected elders, and leaders. We are informed by the words, symbols, and traditions left by those who preceded us or are the current dominant voices in our cultures. This external authority is generally a good thing, but it also represents a cultural trap.

These inherited beliefs may be so numerous and incoherent that we have trouble using them as guides for our lives. If so, some constraint needs to be added. Or, it may be that the assumptions, beliefs, and faith systems are so stifling they need to be loosened.

By using our internal authority, we can stretch our beliefs to consider new ideas, concepts, and data, or we can narrow them to find the ones that are most meaningful for us.

Tips for *loosening* constraints on authority:

- To engage empiricism, inquire about alternative meanings of the words and symbols you value.
- To engage praxis, ask a young person what they think about your beliefs and listen without judgment.
- To engage insight, ask others if they have questions about your cherished beliefs and listen without becoming defensive.
- In general, learn about the beliefs and traditions of other cultures.
- In general, engage with persons in your faith tradition who are liberal or conservative (whatever you are not) with an open mind.
- In general, read more deeply into the origins of your traditions, especially the conflicts.
- In general, learn to balance the amount of importance you place on external authority with your own independent internal authority.

Tips for *tightening* constraints on authority:

- To engage empiricism, clarify the meaning of the words and symbols you value.
- To engage praxis, ask respected elders how they practice their beliefs.
- To engage insight, focus on what excites you about your cherished beliefs.
- In general, learn more about the beliefs and traditions of your culture.
- In general, engage with persons in your faith tradition whose thinking is similar to your own.
- In general, inquire why others are loyal to your traditions.
- In general, articulate what is good and valuable about the external authorities in your context and assimilate that wisdom into the judgments of your informal authority.

Empiricism

Grandpa Jones was fortunate to have resources to fund the gold-mining venture. This made possible the equipment and material support and also the means to measure the depth of the soil over the bedrock, the temperature, and the weather forecast.

Impact of Empiricism on Insight: Patricia Pinson (2012) discusses the life of Walter Andersen, a coastal artist from Mississippi who went beyond recording what he saw in nature (figure 3.2) to inquiring about who we are, how nature works, and how we interact with it. Pinson tells how Andersen liked to read at night at the same time sketching images inspired by his reading. She says:

> It was cool and quiet at night—a time to see the words take shape and take one away into another time, another world.

Figure 3.2: World of Nature

Andersen's experience in the world of nature fostered imaginative insights which captured the essence of what his senses had taken in. The reader may think of examples where empirical knowledge can restrict our imagination, but I love the positive example of Walter Andersen.

Impact of Empiricism on Authority: Science has revealed that the universe is intelligible and mathematically beautiful. The universe is also finely tuned with a subtle balance of expansion and gravity, a balance of gravity and electromagnetism, and a balance of nuclear forces and electromagnetic force. This suggests a dynamic, emergent, self-actualizing universe, moving toward greater complexity and purpose. The hypotheses derived from this empirical reality have replaced many of the hypotheses of the older sciences.

Impact of Empiricism on Praxis: Persons who have made discoveries in the empirical mode inevitably test them (or have others test them) in the mode of praxis. Think of the Wright brothers. Evidence-based conclusions and decisions need to be tested. Practical wisdom emerges when the constraints of the laboratory and specifications are put into action where there are countless compounding variables that can impact the result. When put to the test the empirical truths are either confirmed or disproved.

Empirical knowledge is needed by sailors to guide their actions. Think of sailors needing a compass or the stars (and now GPS) to steer them right. Obtaining the facts can confirm either that correct action is being taken or that the ship is way off course.

> *Example*: Animal biologists who have discovered patterns of behavior that appear to help propagate an endangered species give the information to persons at animal shelters who then create strategies to increase the numbers of the species in the wild.

Trial and error and learning from failure is a way of learning. Failure from evolutional evidence is feedback about the wrong turns we have made.

Reflection on the Power of Empiricism: The data of empiricism can shift our attention in any of the other three modes. It can move us to flights of imagination, to a greater willingness to take risks in order to learn, and to significant changes in our paradigms and worldviews.

This mode gives us assurance that assumptions have been tested and found to be empirically true. The collected empirical data and reason of others to describe reality provides us with predictable and orderly knowledge. We can use this knowledge to plan our lives and direct our actions. Empiricism helps us raise provocative questions, hold on to paradoxes, and welcome "both/and" solutions, rather than the "either/or" often posed by authority. However, as with the other modes, we can get stuck here.

Tips for *loosening* constraints on empiricism:

- To engage authority, read experts who disagree with your way of analyzing data and try to articulate their point of view in an unbiased way.
- To engage praxis, use a form of measurement or data collection you have never tried before.
- To engage insight, define a problem you want to investigate, come up with a hunch on how it will turn out and where the hunch came from, and then do the data collection.
- In general, engage in "what if" thinking.
- In general, collect more data before concluding.
- In general, raise questions about the context of your observations, e.g. is it large enough?

- In general, engage in activities that engage the right brain such as art, music, hiking, meditation, or tai chi.

Tips for *tightening* constraints on empiricism:

- To engage authority, identify your important assumptions on how the world works and survey experts to see how many support them.
- To engage praxis, design an experiment to determine whether one of your assumptions is factually supported.
- To engage insight, use your insight to see the patterns in what you are investigating.
- In general, don't second-guess yourself so much.
- In general, realize that you probably have gathered enough data to make a decision.
- In general, assume that you have a good enough context for your observations.
- In general, engage in activities that stimulate your left brain such as Sudoku, logic and crossword puzzles, using a telescope, or even a junior chemistry set.

PRAXIS

All of the hopes, plans, resources, and data that Grandpa Jones had would have gone nowhere without the enthusiastic participation of his grandsons. Their zeal and dedication to take on a tough task finally brought the gold home.

Impact of Praxis on Insight: What we learn by acting can open up new vistas, new imaginative understandings of the world. For example, the practical tests on animals in enclosures give animal biologists ideas for learning about their behavior in the wild. Those insights then lead to further tests in the laboratory.

To explain the influence of praxis on insight we turn again to the life of Walter Andersen (Pinson, 2012). Pinson writes:

Figure 3.3: Flying Owl

He sought to become one with the creature he saw—not merely an observer but a participant in its life. He said: "The heart is the thing that counts, the mingling of my heart with the heart of the wild bird: to become one with the thing I see" (p 183).

Andersen's sense of interdependence with nature and his participation with it led to his mystical insights and revelations about wholeness. He most often drew pictures of birds (figure 3.3). The capability of flight made them seem symbolic of his spiritual quest. He is noted as saying that the soaring quality of both spirit and intellect show that air and spirit are one.

It is possible that engagement with life could dull one's insights. I am mindful of Thomas Hobbes (1651) statement: "the life of man, solitary, poore (sic), nasty, brutish, and short," but I wish to soar with Andersen.

Impact of Praxis on Authority: We make changes in our beliefs and shift directions as is necessary to be integrated, relevant, and productive. In the process the beliefs are either weakened or strengthened. We may take comfort from recollecting the wonderful lives of our parents or grandparents, but we may need a new set of rules to thrive today.

> *Example*: The inherited and conventional knowledge about animal behavior, to be relevant, needs to be tested in the stressed environments the animals live in today. These tests help build hypotheses that will aid future research to improve the quality of life for both the animals and humans.

Bruce Sanguin (February, 2014) argues that crises provoke the emergence of new and necessary intelligences required to transcend the crisis and become the new thing Spirit is doing in the world.

The crises in the sweep of Big History[11] can be seen as producing a collective wisdom that enabled our species to carry on. The saying "that which doesn't kill us, makes us stronger" comes to mind. Of course this is a sweeping generalization. There are also cases where actions precipitated by a crisis have led to theories that are not life-affirming, such as the internment of all Japanese people during World War II, which "justified" cultural biases through the Viet Nam war and beyond.

Impact of Praxis on Empiricism: One more time we turn to Walter Andersen (Pinson, 2012) to explain the influence of Praxis on Empiricism. Andersen's senses and engagement with nature (praxis) led him to look for evidence of how things are related. He said:

> The strange thing is that the senses tell me the same things that Einstein's equations told him … It means that everything is one (p. 190).

Participation in trial and error generates a lot of data which is grist for the empirical mill. In contemporary science, experience in praxis is vital to construct the models and simulations of our physical world.

---

11 Big History is a multidisciplinary field of historical study which explores human existence in the past across the maximum time scale from the Big Bang to the present. Empirical evidence is used to study the cosmos, earth, the emergence of life, and humanity. The emerging field is taught at universities and secondary schools.

Reflections on the Power of Praxis: Praxis opens up new possibilities for a mystical approach to the world, for developing new theories and hypotheses, and for refining our data about reality. Learning through action, including what we learn from our bodies, may be the undervalued way of knowing that has been confined to religion, the arts, and the humanities but is now seen as a valuable ally to science.

In this mode we learn by acting on and personally experiencing what we know from the other modes. This learning is reinforced if the outcomes are what we expect or are appropriate. For example, we act to achieve our goals and life's purpose. The positive outcomes of these actions can lock us into a set routine of practices that may need correction. We can test whether our purpose is still relevant and life-giving by finding out what others are discovering, what new theories are emerging, and what our insights are saying to us.

Tips for *loosening* constraints in praxis:

- To engage empiricism, find new ways to do some action you do all the time, collect data, make a hypothesis, and try out the new action.
- To engage authority, study what others have said and/or written about other ways of doing what you already know how to do.
- To engage insight, question whether your actions are life-giving and compassionate.
- In general, try to be less predictable or routine in what you do or say.
- In general, venture into new areas.
- In general, make more time to be silent and reflect.

Tips for *tightening* constraints in praxis:

- To engage empiricism, collect data on two or three of the ways you do things, compare the data, and pick one method for a set time.
- To engage authority, select one expert opinion about your endeavors and adhere to that system.
- To engage insight, trust yourself, that your actions are life-giving and compassionate.
- In general, strive to be more predictable in your actions; develop a routine.
- In general, stick to what you know best.
- In general, act as soon as you know what you want to do, don't procrastinate or look for other options.

SUMMARY

The mutual interaction of each of the four ways of knowing, while usually done as a matter of course, can also benefit from more intentionality.

It is worthwhile to check to see how the modes positively influence each other and what they can contribute to our daily lives. When we experience dissonance, we can also dig deeper into understanding how the modes may be cancelling each other.

Each of our modes may be too constrained or too unconstrained. We can ask if they need to be loosened or tightened. We can see if we are focused on what is significant—does it matter? We can make our contacts across the modes of knowing longer, deeper, broader, or narrower. Any changes we make in one mode will affect the others.

In the next chapter the interaction of the modes is taken to a new level. When all four modes interact, it is likely that new creative and deeper understandings of reality will emerge.

QUESTIONS FOR REFLECTION

1. As you reflect on your ways of knowing, do you need to loosen or broaden how you hold or constrict each way of knowing? Or do you need to tighten or narrow your focus on each way of knowing?

2. As you engage each way of knowing, are you focused on important differences, that is, the aspects that will generate new or deeper knowledge? Or do you not pay sufficient attention to what is important?

3. Are your communications and contacts in each way of knowing transformative? Are they long, deep, and heartfelt enough to change your understanding, or are they superficial so nothing ever changes?

POSSIBLE ACTIONS

1. Review the tips for loosening and tightening constraints in *one* of the four modes.

    A.   Choose one tip for that mode and implement it.

    B.   Record your observations and feelings about what happened.

    C.   Choose a second tip for your to-do list.

2. Choose one tip from another mode and repeat the steps in #1.

3. Continue likewise for the remaining two modes and repeat the steps in #1.

CHAPTER 4

Creative Interaction

To this point the focus has been on the four modes of knowing and their interaction—one with another. In this chapter the simultaneous interaction of all four modes and the possibilities of the emergence of new knowledge are discussed. When all four modes interact, each mode is altered by the impact of the other modes and greater complexities and new truths emerge.

To explain how the four modes can interact to produce surprising, creative new understandings of reality, it is useful to develop a model.

CRITERIA FOR A "GOOD ENOUGH"[12] MODEL

There are many theories of knowing (Pinker, 1997; Morin, 2008; Mitchell, 2009; Evers, 2010; Dew, 2014), but none provides a practical model for integrating the multiple ways of knowing. The model presented in this chapter meets three criteria that are essential for a model of knowing that can guide action: interconnected, durable, and dynamical.

1 Interconnected

Kegan (1982, 1994) has described how we have developed complex levels of knowing and consciousness. He argues that a model of knowing capable of dealing with current complex issues requires a stage of consciousness that sees the interconnection of all aspects of reality.

2 Durable

A durable model is interesting and useful (Jinkins, 2014). It is

1. *Vivid and clear.* It is readily understandable, memorable, and maybe even visual.
2. *Adaptable.* It can be applied in a number of different contexts and used to analyze many subjects.

---

12 "Good enough" is actually a technical term in complexity science referring to adopting minimal specifications that produce the desired outcomes rather than specifying maximum rules and procedures that limit the flexibility necessary to adapt to novel situations.

3. *Able to re-orient our thinking.* It may shock us out of our usual way of seeing things by framing the questions differently.

4. *Generative.* It evokes or provokes conversation about persistent concerns.

5. *Heuristic.* It is a tool for us to use to investigate a subject and to understand it better and more deeply.

3 Dynamical

For new knowledge and new patterns[13] of understanding to emerge from using the model, it must be dynamical.[14] The dynamics and interaction of the various aspects of the model are so unknowable that the effects and outcomes of the interactions cannot be predicted.

MAKING THE WAYS OF KNOWING MODEL

In the gold mining story, Johnny learned that a good approximation of truth can be found by accessing multiple ways of knowing. That example (figure 4.1) is useful to present the Ways of Knowing Model. Mining gold, the metaphor for finding truth, required two dimensions of knowing. In the Model the dimensions are *perceiving* and *meaning*. Both dimensions portray reality. Both are constructions of our consciousness.

Perceiving refers to how we "see" the world—with our five senses and our ability to know things beyond our five senses—our intuition. This is the vertical axis in the model—*perception*—with its two components of *sensing* and *intuition*.[15]

Figure 4.1: Gold Mining Example of Model

		Meaning	
		Ascribed	**Experienced**
Perception	**Intuition**	*Expert advice on where to mine for gold* (**Authority**)	*A hunch and idea where gold might be* (**Insight**)
	Sensing	*Specific information about the creek bed and the right kind of equipment* (**Empiricism**)	*Willingness to take action* (**Praxis**)

The horizontal dimension is *meaning*,[16] which we either experience ourselves (experienced

---

13 Complexity scientists call these patterns "attractors," an image of an emergent behavior that has a finite boundary and infinite variability within the boundary.

14 Dynamical is one kind of change. It is change that is unknowable in advance because of all of the uncontrollable variations affecting all of the factors involved.

15 This is the same dimension that the Swiss psychologist Carl Jung (1921) discovered many years ago and that was popularized in the Myers-Briggs questionnaire that is widely used in many organizations.

16 This dimension of knowing is from the work of Letiche, Lissack, and Schultz (2011) who discuss the two modes of coherence as ascribed and experienced.

meaning) or is told to us (ascribed meaning). The meaning dimension allows us to understand what our senses and our intuition have told us.

When the two dimensions of knowing are placed on the chart constructed by Johnny's mom, the four ways of knowing are revealed. Figure 4.2 visually depicts how the four ways of knowing can simultaneously interact in the middle space of the circle.

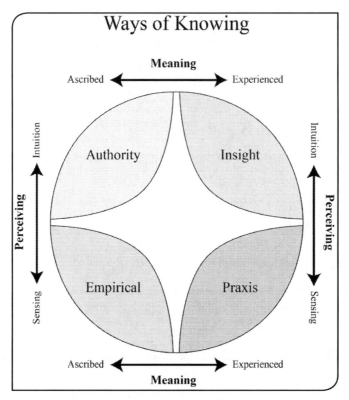

Figure 4.2: Four Ways of Knowing

The model contains aspects of theories of personality, problem-solving, and decision-making. Most of all, it is an epistemological model of the components of knowledge.

In the Apollo 13 story, Woodfill said, "The concept seemed to evolve as all looked on." This was a process in which the four modes interacted to produce a "miracle." The expertise, data, vision, and testing all worked together. By using all four modes in such a fashion, the team became more resilient. They became freer and creative in their thinking and responses and the crew of Apollo 13 was saved. In the context of the Ways of Knowing Model, the interaction was in the middle space of the circle—the zone of self-organizing where order is created from chaos when the conditions are right.

When the four modes interact in a self-organizing process, outcomes emerge that are surprising and unpredictable. In the process of emergence the mode boundaries become permeable, the "truth," or reality, of one mode is modified, and an enriched environment promotes learning and growth. As all four modes interact we see reality from multiple perspectives. We are more likely to discover what is important and true to us and others. We are more likely to "find gold."

Barfield (1965) defines an idol as anything that does not participate in life apart from its own separate life. Idolatry privileges an idol above all other facets of life. Applying that definition of idolatry to the four modes of knowing, any single mode that does not interact with other modes is idolatrous. That is a rather strong assertion, but it is not unlike Jung's warning of "one-sidedness." Using all four modes in the self-organizing space greatly reduces the possibility of idolatry. I will amplify that argument later, but first, let's consider how "emergence" explains the outcome of multiple mode interactions.

EMERGENCE

The concept of emergence[17] in the physical sciences describes how new, novel, complex wholes arise from the interaction of the parts. The new whole is not explainable, reducible to, or predictable from their simpler, more fundamental components. For example, in biological research scientists have found that only 5 percent of the variation from person to person can be explained by our genes.

As we saw in chapter 3, when one mode interacts with another, the conflicting perspectives about what is true can be reconciled. The modes can support each other, even though they are in apparent conflict. Each contributes to the whole and keeps us from the one-sidedness and idolatry described earlier.

When the four modes interact, we can expect even more creativity arising with surprising unimaginable outcomes. Figure 4.3 suggests this unpredictable dynamic of emergence.

Figure 4.3: Dynamical Nature of Emergence

---

17 The term *emergent* was coined by the pioneer psychologist G. H. Lewes (1875) who stated that emergents cooperate by adding things of unlike kinds; the emergent is unlike its components and it cannot be reduced to its sum or its difference. Generally emergence refers to the development of novel and coherent structures, patterns, and properties.

Emergence can be either considered as a *process* of knowing or as a *property* of the learning process (Lichtenstein, 2014).[18] As the four modes interact, the results are unpredictable in detail. The interaction of different modes of knowing is a process of self-organizing where new novel combinations and patterns occur as information is exchanged and new actions and adaptations occur. Disorder is created, leading ultimately to some new unpredictable order that stays stable for a while and then changes, often dramatically.[19]

GENERATIVE EMERGENCE

The emergence that occurs in the interaction of the four modes may be similar to the "generative emergence" in human systems that Lichtenstein (2014) describes. In generative emergence, the emergent property or action is intentional. The emergence is initiated by a desire, goal, passion, opportunity, or an aspiration to affect the situation in some specific way. The original direction is never the end result because of the dynamics of feedback and experimentation that happen in emergence.

Lichtenstein describes the process of generative emergence as a cycle of five interdependent phases. The cycle is initiated by (1) opportunity tension, which gives rise to (2) disequilibrium, stress, and experiments. If these qualities continue to increase, (3) the changes are amplified to a critical threshold, an event that signals a tipping point of emergence. This threshold (4) generates a new emergent order through the recombination of components, as well as a stabilization of the situation itself. If adaptive, (5) the emergent order will be sustainable; if not, the emergent order will dissolve or change enough to co-exist with its environment.

The following example about deciding what college to attend applies Lichtenstein's five-step cycle to the Ways of Knowing Model:

Figure 4.4: College Selection

---

18   For example, an amoeba, as a complex organization of molecules, has properties that do not exist in the molecules themselves. The amoeba's activity is an emergent property (Jeeves and Brown, 2012). As a process in human systems, emergents arise from the interactions based on "simple rules" that no single person directs. The dynamics are a kind of "black box"—no general mechanisms have been identified to explain how these emergents emerge.

19   Gladwell (2002) popularized this notion as the "tipping point." Small causes or fluctuations can have a huge, unpredictable effect on knowledge that is "far from equilibrium." The innovation and novelty can be thought about as a self-organizing process, an emergent, repetitive but unpredictable pattern of energy. In some instances, those involved will view it as a disaster. Others will see the same situation as an opportunity.

1. *Opportunity tension.* "Joe" is faced with a decision (figure 4.4) about what college to attend upon graduating from high school. He is considering a local college in New York where he lives, several in the Midwest, and one in California.

2. *Disequilibrium, stress, and experiments.* Joe experiences conflicting advice from parents who want him to stay locally (authority), relevant facts about the colleges' strengths (empiricism), his fantasy about where he will be most happy (insight), and impressions from field trips to experience each campus (praxis).

3. *Amplification of changes to a tipping point.* The deadline for sending an acceptance letter approaches and Joe considers the knowledge he has gained from each way of knowing.

4. *An emergent order is generated through the recombination of components and the situation is stabilized.* Joe chooses the California college. His insight about where he will be most happy provided the tipping point. Perhaps the additional information that his girlfriend will also be attending there amplified his insight.

5. *If adaptive, the emergent order is sustained.* Assuming the information from each mode reinforces his decision and roadblocks do not emerge (e.g. parents withhold money for out-of-state tuition and traveling), Joe will attend the college in California.

This example fits the Lichtenstein model of generative emergence because the emergent order (Joe choosing a college) was intentional. The process was structured so there was a high probability that there would be one of several previously identified outcomes.

In the process of emergence described in the next section, the probability of a certain outcome cannot be predicted.

CREATIVE EMERGENCE

The self-organizing space where the four modes interact, creative emergence, (figure 4.5) is broader than generative emergence in the sense that its outcomes may or may not lead to the material outcomes or new order that Lichtenstein suggests. In creative emergence, the information from the ways of knowing blend and become a singularity. The person experiencing creative emergence reveals the pattern/

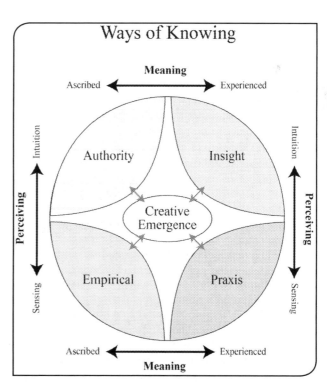

Figure 4.5: Creative Emergence

order that is emerging. Whether the person is a writer, artist, dancer, worker, student, etc., the new pattern emerges through them.

In creative emergence the modes of learning are held in opposition.[20] Contact is made between the modes by asking questions, welcoming differences, noticing rather than judging, and maintaining a position that holds "both/and" and "either/or" as possible outcomes. By holding opposite positions in creative tension, it is likely that the positions will be transcended as new knowledge forms. Jung called this the "transcendent function" (Olson, 1990).

Unlike the example of choosing a college, wherein the parameters are set to lead to one choice among several known options, in creative emergence knowledge arises that goes beyond the bounds of the four modes. When there is genuine contact across all modes, something new emerges. The creative dissonance shakes and stirs the content of each mode. In our college example, it may mean that Joe postpones going to college, perhaps pursuing a sport or artistic interest and continues his education on a part-time basis, or on-line, or maybe even years later, or never. In creative emergence we interact with a mix of our intuition, our senses, ascribed meaning, and experienced meaning. The outcome is unpredictable.

In creative emergence there is convergence, reconciliation, and enrichment. New thoughts come to and through us. We achieve a new balance in our understanding and even in our way of life. Old paradoxes and polarities are resolved. Some new paradoxes and polarities may be created.

METAPHOR FOR CREATIVE EMERGENCE: IMPROVISATIONAL THEATER

Figure 4.6: Improv Theater

An improvisational (improv) theater metaphor (figure 4.6) illustrates how new possibilities emerge from the complex mix of interactions among the improv actors.

Each of the actors is autonomous. They interact as they perform. The place, time, duration, rules, and parameters have been set (*empiricism*). They know the theory and practice of improv theater (*authority*). They use their imagination and fantasy (*insight*). They act on their desire to learn and do something useful (*praxis*). They start anywhere.

They listen to each other and adapt to create the story. Each member influences the other

---

20 Through the lens of creative emergence we come to understand our inner lives as a self-organized, novel reality that both transcends and includes our outer life. The interplay of the four ways of knowing builds both our inner and our outer lives. R. Klein (2010) argues that our sense of self emerges from the interaction of different perspectives. Klein sees relational selfhood as an experiential dimension that is a neural function of the brain.

members of the group and the audience. The audience, in turn, influences the members with laughter, boos, and applause. Insecurity is expected, mistakes are made, interactions build on each other, and meaning and significance emerge (*creative emergence*).

The quality and creativity of the performance depend on all of these complex interactions. The emerging patterns of comedy or drama, in turn, affect the performance on the next and successive interactions. Each performance is unique, but patterns are apparent.

For us to engage in the kind of dialogue that will trigger creative emergence, we must be ready to receive information and feedback that may contradict our deeply held beliefs and be open to scrutiny and consideration of opposing views. O'Dea (2012, p. 162) says that such dialogue "allows people to experience community, share the exploration of ideas, evolve new kinds of consensus where none existed before, and create fields of collective resonance."

Creative emergence also requires narrative. Telling stories allows us to reframe and transform our intuitions and senses into something coherent for us and others (Letiche, Lissack, pp 38–41). In our college example, Joe needs a story he can tell all of the stakeholders in the decision, including his parents, girlfriend, and peers.

The creative emergence process (figure 4.5) suggests that to move into the inner circle we need to "dance" the wheel. Consider Native peoples' practice of moving to different parts of a medicine wheel to gain strength, courage, insight, etc. (Loomis, 1991). We need to pull into the dance of learning, relationships, and creativity from all four modes.

Creative emergence describes how the universe actually works (Reho, 2013–14). In the universe as a whole and in our biosphere, creative emergence processes drive the cosmos forward. Bruce Sanguin (2008) says there are three principals involved: novelty, self-organization, and transcendence/inclusion.

1. *Novelty* tells us that as the universe continues to develop along new and uncharted horizons, it makes it up as it goes along. The results are surprising, unpredictable, and move toward greater diversity as well as complexity.

2. We have already seen how *self-organizing* occurs when the four modes are brought together in pursuit of a common purpose. The Apollo 13 crew created greater complexity (the "contraption") and greater consciousness (sense that Houston needed to create a "miracle").

3. The principles of *inclusion and transcendence* work together to ensure that the best of the past is carried forward in the very process of moving beyond the past. The essential information from any mode of knowing is not lost as it creatively merges with the other modes to form greater complexity.

The parable of the *Good Samaritan* illustrates the surprising, unpredictable process and outcomes of creative emergence using the four ways of knowing.

GOOD SAMARITAN PARABLE

There was once a man traveling from Jerusalem to Jericho. On the way he was attacked by robbers. They took his clothes, beat him up, and went off leaving him half-dead. Luckily, a priest was on his way down the same road, but when he saw him he angled across to the other side. Then a Levite religious man showed up; he also avoided the injured man. A Samaritan traveling the road came on him. When he saw the man's condition, his heart went out to him. He gave him first-aid, disinfecting and bandaging his wounds. Then he lifted him onto his donkey, led him to an inn, and made him comfortable. In the morning he took out two silver coins and gave them to the innkeeper, saying, "Take good care of him. If it costs any more, put it on my bill—I'll pay you on my way back."

Luke 10:30b–35 from *The Message,* Eugene Peterson

Figure 4.7: The Good Samaritan

INTRODUCTION

The parable is about the willingness and ability to see a person in need and respond (figure 4.7). It is a hero story and, as such, the audience of such a story expects to identify with the hero. But in this narrative it is very difficult for a first-century Jewish audience to identify with a Samaritan, whom the Jews despised (Scott, 2001).

Insight

The Samaritan may not have expected to have this response to an injured man on the side of the road, but the sight of the naked and bleeding man churned the Samaritan's guts inside him with such ferocity that it simply obliterated the walls that culturally separated him from a supposed enemy (Holloway, 2003). This gut churning is an example of the ambiguity that insight can bring to creative emergence. As the Samaritan's guts churned there were a number of possibilities. He could choose to walk away, call others for help, kill the man, or give assistance. He chose to resolve his ambiguity by taking care of a person who was not only different from him but who was also a sworn enemy.

Authority

The Samaritan certainly knew the law and the conventional moral codes of the time. To help the injured man that the Samaritan culture stigmatized as an archenemy, the Samaritan had to draw upon a different authority, a new moral world. Scott (2001) says the Samaritan acted out of a moral world in which the map of human relations is reorganized, where a despised foreigner can be placed in the center of the new moral map.

Empiricism

The phrase "when he saw him" shows up three times in the parable. They all "saw" the man's condition, but only the Samaritan responds. They all understood the man's situation, they all had the same data, but only one acted to remedy it. For empiricism to participate in creative emergence there must be a readiness to see things as they are, expect surprises, and be ready to interpret incoming data in new ways.

Praxis

The actions of the Samaritan in giving first aid to the injured man, disinfecting and bandaging wounds, lifting him onto a donkey and taking him to an inn, certainly brought the Samaritan in close physical contact. In those actions he must have learned much about the injured man and about himself. He was flexible, adaptable, maneuverable, and ready to improvise.

Creative Emergence

To self-organize in creative emergence, a degree of uncertainty is necessary in order to consider new information. If too constrained, we stay locked into the status quo. The parable moved its audience (us) from a space of certainty (Jews and Samaritans have nothing to do with each other) to a self-organizing place of new information where change is possible.

In this parable Jesus presented a new way of relating to reality. We should expect grace, change, mercy, and aid to come from unexpected sources at unexpected times. The parable shows that moral codes are provisional and can be discarded when faced with the ambiguity of new situations. Creative emergence is about letting go of certainty about our rules and worldviews and taking risks.

The creative emergence space created by the parable reverses the questions we usually ask. Thielicke (1960, p.168) says: "We shall ask not 'Who is my neighbor?' but 'To whom am I a neighbor? Who is laid at my door? Who is expecting help from me and who looks upon me as his neighbor?' This reversal of the question is precisely the point of the parable."

Nolan (2006, p. 54) says that, "To appreciate the impact the Samaritan story must have had on Jesus's contemporaries, we might retell it as the story of an injured Christian soldier who is helped by a Muslim fundamentalist while a Christian military chaplain and a Christian social worker walk by on the other side." Nolan concludes that seeing the world from the bottom up is humbling—to know what it is to need and receive aid from our enemy, as well as to give aid to someone we have always tried to avoid.

SUMMARY

The Ways of Knowing Model has two dimensions: perceiving (including sensing and intuition) and meaning (including experienced meaning and ascribed meaning). When put in a two-by-two matrix the dimensions encompass the four ways of knowing (insight, authority, empiricism, and praxis).

The Model meets three criteria of an effective model: *interconnection*—all aspects of reality must be seen as being interrelated and as part of a whole; *durability*—the various ways of knowing and discussing the subject are interesting and useful; and *dynamical*—new patterns of knowledge creation are possible.

The Model combines aspects of theories of personality, problem-solving, decision-making, and epistemology. All four modes contribute to our capacity to test our knowledge for truthfulness.

In creative emergence we need to let go of the certainty of old ways of thinking and be more flexible, adaptive, and ready to improvise. If we are tied to only a few ways of knowing it is difficult to act upon the new possibilities that are open to us.

Kauffman (2008) describes our untapped potential as the *adjacent possible*. To survive in a changing environment, we need to evolve to a higher level of complexity, to what is possible for us given our limitations and the environment surrounding us. In creative emergence we can improvise and move to our adjacent possible, as did the Samaritan.

In creative emergence exciting outcomes emerge from opening up to all ways of knowing. In previous chapters the dangers of relying on one way of knowing and how each way of knowing can either add value or detract from the other modes were discussed. In this chapter, putting all four ways of knowing into a self-organizing space led to unexpected and totally novel outcomes. This creative emergence is the hope for overcoming the usual one-sided approach to the complex problems which had made Barfield (1965) pessimistic about the future.

In chapters 5 and 6 the model is applied to overcome one-sidedness in areas of interest to the reader and in our organizations and societies.

QUESTIONS FOR REFLECTION

1. How did the solution self-organize and "emerge" for the Apollo 13 crew? Which of the four ways of knowing was most important?

2. In generative emergence, a process is structured to engage the four ways of knowing to produce an outcome. Do you have an example where you have used a similar process?

3. In creative emergence, the outcome is uncertain and often surprising, as in the *Good Samaritan* parable. In what aspects of your life would simultaneously engaging all four ways of knowing be especially valuable?

POSSIBLE ACTIONS

1. Go to a busy intersection of roads or sidewalks and observe processes of self-organizing. Notice how patterns of people or cars form and dissipate, particularly:

    a.   What provides a container or boundary for the patterns, e.g. traffic light?

    b.   What are apparent conflicts?

    c.   What interactions are important in resolving those conflicts?

    You will be observing how creative emergence works as new patterns within the space form and change. Note how all four modes of knowing are involved.

2. Choose a difficult problem facing you or your organization. Convene a small group or team and, from the perspective of each way of knowing, brainstorm four lists of aspects of the problem. Ask the group to review the four lists and see what emerges from the group that reframes or solves the problem.

CHAPTER 5
Taking Adaptive Action

In the previous chapters the following uses of the Ways of Knowing Model were demonstrated.

- To raise awareness that there are two dimensions and four alternative ways of knowing (chapters 1 and 2).
- To overcome one-sidedness by changing the constraints on the ways of knowing and how they interact with one another (chapter 3).
- To create the possibility of creative emergence by moving the ways of knowing into a self-organizing process (chapter 4).

This chapter introduces adaptive action questions as a means of applying the Ways of Knowing Model to daily living issues and topics of interest.

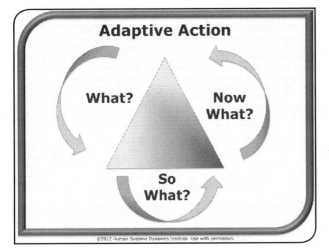

Figure 5.1: Adaptive Action

ADAPTIVE ACTION

The three questions of Adaptive Action (Eoyang and Holladay, 2013) are:

What?
So What?
Now What?

Everyone experiences adaptive action.[21] We notice *what* is happening.

---

21 In the 1920s, Cardinal Joseph Cardijn in Belgium organized poor workers into an organization that now is found in fifty countries of the world. They became known as the "Jocists," a name derived from the initials of the movement, J. O. C in French and Spanish (Young Christian Workers in English). His method comprised three actions to apply in judging social conditions: see, judge, and act, similar to what, so what, and now what. Bob Luther, who provided this example, says, "There is nothing new under the sun," a quote from Ecclesiastes 1:9, which is about three thousand years old.

We discern its importance by asking *so what?* We then decide *now what* action to take. As we assess the impact of the now-what decision, we are once again taking notice, bringing us back to *what*. Adaptive action is a positive feedback process that helps us choose where to start, what to influence, and what to do after we see the impact of our influence.

WHAT?

By answering the *what* question we become aware and attentive to whatever each way of knowing is offering. Asking what lets us discern what is happening and what needs to change. We question our assumptions, consider other perspectives, and inquire to reveal the complexity of the present. *What* helps us notice opportunities we might have missed.

What focuses us on the conditions that generated the patterns we observe. We can contact others who can help describe, name, and explain the *what*.

SO WHAT?

The *so what* question allows us to assess the meaning and significance of the knowledge each way of knowing has yielded. We discern what matters to you, us, others, and what opportunities are emerging. We focus on differences that are important but may not be recognized. *So what* breaks through habits and assumptions so we can explore opportunities we never would have imagined.

Exploring *so what* is best done in dialogue and shared conversation. We must be curious about the affirmations and questions of others who are different from us. Use questions to sort, categorize, select, and discard information until meaning emerges.

NOW WHAT?

The *now what* question helps us determine an appropriate course of action. *Now what* moves us out of helplessness and into action. As we act, the patterns around us shift and we can begin the cycle of inquiry again.

The actions in the now-what phase depend on specifics of any given situation including the turbulence of the environment and the level of urgency. Developing timelines, reminders, and measures for success will help guide our future inquiry and action and clarify our expectations for who will do what. As the cycle moves through the phases over and over, we evaluate and reevaluate.

If the change was not what we wanted or expected, we can learn from failure and start the cycle again by returning to *what*.

Each phase of the adaptive action cycle is informed by each of the four ways of knowing—our perception of reality, the wisdom our belief systems bring to bear, our insights, and the practical actions we can take. We see what we can see (*what*), weigh what we cannot fully know (*so what*) and choose some kind of action, no matter how small (*now what*).

The dynamical change in adaptive action is ongoing, unpredictable, and interdependent. Self-organization and emergence is always happening. Our challenge is to adapt and respond in sustainable and resilient ways.

We can look for answers in the *what* of the new patterns, see new possibilities in the *so what* and try something new in the *now what*.

APPLYING ADAPTIVE ACTION

Analysis of a Daily Life Issue

To demonstrate the usefulness of adaptive action in implementing the Ways of Knowing Model, a specific aspect of personal health—diet and exercise—will be analyzed. In table 5.1 there are some specific adaptive action questions about the topic for each of the four modes. The overall general questions are:

- Am I accessing the knowledge in all four modes in dealing with my diet and exercise issues?
- What can I do to adjust the constraints in the modes to increase the possibility of creative emergence?
- What is the current situation regarding my own diet and exercise plan? So what needs to be improved, if anything? Now what will I do?

Even a small change can have a big impact on the other ways of knowing. Change in any one mode will move you into the possibility of creative emergence. For example, just deciding to start an exercise program in a gym (praxis) can impact our sense of the importance of diet and exercise (insight), make us curious about what a physical training expert would recommend (authority) and quicken a desire to learn more about new data on diet and exercise (empirical). Or we may just choose to listen to Dr. Oz and learn all of his ways of knowing about diet, exercise, and health.

Persons acquainted with or interested in the CDE Model (Olson & Eoyang, 2001; Eoyang and Holladay, 2013) are encouraged to read Appendix A: The CDE Model and Ways of Knowing, which explains how the use of all four modes can be enhanced by changing the conditions (Container, Difference, or Exchange) that allow a situation to self-organize. Changing just *one* of the conditions in only *one* of the modes can have a significant impact on the other modes.

Table 5.1: Application to a Daily Life Issue

Authority	Insight
What feedback and advice have I received from my friends and doctors about my weight and fitness? **So What** of this feedback and advice should I accept? **Now What** can I do to incorporate this feedback and advice into my daily life?	**What** is my ideal weight and physical ability for my age? **So What** is the difference between the ideal and where I am in it? **Now What** goals can I achieve that will reduce the difference?
Empirical	**Praxis**
What is the current scientific information about dieting and exercise? **So What** is the information that is pertinent for me? **Now What** can I do to use this information?	**What** am I currently doing to optimize my weight and fitness? **So What** has been the result? **Now What** action can I take to make progress?

EXPLORATION OF A TOPIC OF INTEREST

The Model could be applied to any topic using adaptive action questions. The example I will use has stirred controversy in the science-religion dialogue. The term *sacred*, a concept usually associated only with religion and spirituality, has recently begun to be used in areas of science.[22]

WHAT IS THE MEANING OF "THE SACRED"

Insight

Using this mode of experienced intuition, the sacred is experience that points to something, somewhere, sometime, or someone beyond the experience itself. We may experience unity in epiphanies, flashes of understanding, whether we are awake and meditating, when in an altered state of consciousness, or when dreaming. Some might call this "the force" or the "breath of God."

Authority

As a species we collectively made sense of the insights about the "something more" and developed sets of beliefs and religions. Much of this inherited wisdom about the sacred is based on scriptures and persons deemed to be holy with special knowledge of the divine. Many of the beliefs are about the

---

22 Stuart Kaufman (2008) and Adam Frank (2010) use the term *sacred* to describe the awe and wonder they experience in learning about the biosphere and cosmos.

sacredness of creation, that hope is real, and that we are destined for somewhere good.

Empiricism

We perceive that everything is connected in relationships of living energy and intricate patterns of information. The universe, galaxies, stars, planets, animals, plants, molecules, atoms, quarks, and subquarks all are aspects of the natural and material world that we can consider to be sacred.

Praxis

As we act on our perceptions and experience in the material world, we find that our behavior affects everything. We experience the energy of the universe flowing through us as we meditate and pray. We have an evolutionary impulse to find the sacred and co-create with the divine.

So What?

Creative Emergence

When we actively engage all four ways of knowing, incorporating knowledge from both science and religion, we can let go of constraints of how to understand mystery and engage the sacred. Paradoxes become reconciled (or they become tolerable and even engaging).

Now What?

There is a positive difference in how we act toward nature, the earth, our fellow humans, and other species.

Avoiding Traps in Adaptive Action

Even the best use of adaptive action can derail when judgment, defensiveness, or conflict cloud our perceptions. If my answers to *what, so what,* and *now what* focus on the worst in others, defending myself, or reinforcing conflict, then adaptive action merely strengthens patterns that enslave me. To avoid these traps, Eoyang and Holladay (2013) suggest three very simple rules.

Rule 1: Turn judgment into curiosity. Judgment, even when it is true, blocks choice. It locks us into anger or bias. At the same time, it limits the amount of freedom we are willing to give to others.

Rule 2: Turn defensiveness into self-reflection. Fear leads me to retreat, dig in, avoid engagement, and focus on building or maintaining boundaries to defend myself. Those boundaries hold me hostage because they restrain the very freedom they were designed to create. While I need to be safe, I also can explore other, more freeing ways to meet basic needs. I expand my horizons when I reflect on my own capacity to grow in new ways and to see and act differently.

Rule 3: Turn conflict into shared inquiry. When we choose conflict—especially conflict that is prolonged and profound—we choose slavery. Whatever we invest in anger and offensive action, we steal from positive passion and possibility. Even when our enemies are not immediately willing to share in inquiry, we can increase our own freedom by opening opportunities for dialogue. We ask ourselves, "*What* is a question that we can pursue together? *So what* options for action might serve us both? *Now what* path will lead us forward together?"

SUMMARY

Adaptive action approaches are meant to stimulate your own ideas of how best to apply the Ways of Knowing Model. Everyone is unique. Using new ways of knowing and activating creative emergence will differ for every person and for every sphere of activity.

You may identify a person you admire to see how he or she uses the multiple ways of knowing. Comparing those patterns to your own preferences may be useful. You should also be able to explore aspects of daily life and apply the Model to topics of special interest. Applying the methods in a group or team is especially helpful in developing new ways of using each mode.

The next chapter explores how using the concepts and tools presented in the book can foster a deeper understanding of the epistemological bases of assumptions, the presence and force of archetypal patterns, and how a sense of purpose is developed. Why have we developed these capabilities of knowing that are unique to our species? Are they meant to lead us into a future of wholeness and connectedness of which mystics have foretold for centuries?

QUESTIONS FOR REFLECTION

Use adaptive action (*what, so what, now what*) to analyze your scores on the self-assessment.

1. *What* is the pattern you have discovered? Do you agree with the pattern?

2. *So what* does this mean to you?

3. *Now what* do you want to do: change the pattern or reinforce it?

POSSIBLE ACTIONS

1. Choose some issue or topic of interest to you and discuss it with others using all four ways of knowing. For each way of knowing ask *what, so what, and now what.*

2. Convene a group to discuss a significant issue.

    a.   Use the Ways of Knowing Model to identify multiple aspects of the issue using *what* questions.

    b.   As a group, reflect on what has been discussed and ask *so what* questions.

    c.   Identify the most important so-what aspects.

    d.   Discuss *now what*. What are the actions that the group believes should be taken?

CHAPTER 6

Finding Reality

In this chapter the metaphor of mining is extended to

- examine core assumptions and beliefs;
- manage the archetypes that drive our life stories;
- discover the emergence of purpose;
- explore organizational and societal issues.

CONTRIBUTIONS OF THE MODES

Before considering these four deeper and wider applications of the Ways of Knowing Model, it is useful to review what unleashing each of the modes can positively contribute to this deeper exploration.

Insight

As the gateway to our intuitive experience of what is meaningful, insight, when unfettered in creative emergence, reveals flashes of understanding of both *what is* and *what might be*. Just as dreams are the "royal road to the unconscious" (attributed to Freud), with insight we can tap into the spiritual aspects of life. Insight helps to engage the wisdom of both external and internal authority, provides direction when reviewing empirical data, and helps us to take rapid adaptive action.

Authority

As the way of knowing that bridges collective intuition and ascribed meaning, external authority, when freely interacting in creative emergence, provides an integral understanding of the wisdom that has accumulated for centuries in diverse cultures and circumstances. From ancient maxims to modern scientific theories, what is known through authority provides valuable categories and processes that focus our interactions in creative emergence. This permits us to develop an authentic, well-informed internal authority that productively hones our insights, offers hypotheses to be tested, and provides essential moral guidance.

Empiricism

Empiricism connects ascribed meaning and the reality revealed by the senses and develops mental complexity. The nuances of myriad pieces of information and facts in the empirical realm keep creative emergence connected to material reality. Empiricism fosters imaginative insights, verifies theories generated by authority, and provides theories to be tested by praxis.

Praxis

With praxis we experience meaning through our senses. Praxis, when allowed to impact the other ways of knowing, increases our resilience. We are able to more resolutely act upon our insights, follow where our senses lead us, and engage the wisdom offered by others. Praxis transforms insights into practical reality, tests the theories generated by empiricism, and thereby generates more data to be reviewed by authority.

CORE ASSUMPTIONS

In a search for truth and reality it is necessary to confront the inevitability of biases that color the search.

The domains and disciplines of sciences, arts, humanities, and religions are worldviews that have their own distinctive discourses and languages, their own preferred ways of knowing. Each of these worldviews contributes to an understanding of reality; however, they are "holding environments" for selected ways of knowing (Kegan, 1994). By prizing one or two ways of knowing, any one worldview limits the interplay of multiple ways of knowing and what could emerge from their interaction. A worldview is like looking at reality through a lens that colors everything (figure 6.1).

Figure 6.1: Looking at Reality through a Worldview

For example, a worldview based largely on faith "knows" that there is a reality outside of sensory observation but too often discounts the revelations of science. Conversely, a scientific worldview usually rejects the possibility of knowing anything that cannot be objectively verified, leaving out the contribution of subjective intuition and feelings.[23]

---

23 Soren Kierkegaard, the famous Danish existential philosopher, saw knowledge as both subjective and objective (Piety, 2010). Objective knowledge is interested in reality as a whole and is certain or probable. Subjective knowledge, Kierkegaard's primary concern, is interested in the particularity of the individual and has psychological certainty. Subjective knowledge concerns knowledge of God, self-knowledge, and ethical-religious knowledge and is essentially prescriptive. Objective knowledge is essentially descriptive.

What we know is necessarily limited because of the partial models contained in our worldviews. Our modes of discourse about meaning always reduce the complexity they are trying to describe.

The normative, ethical, social, political, psychological, economic, and religious domains include open, rich, and dynamic interactions at all levels of existence. It is difficult for any model to capture all of this knowledge, including the model presented in this book.

Hákan Snellman (2010),[24] a Swedish physicist, says "real knowledge" is knowledge that is motivating and responsible for supporting life and the biosphere. Snellman argues:

> Real knowledge should be such knowledge that connects man to his home in the cosmos and also to his purpose on this earth. When knowledge is responsibility, it asks of us to build it on care for the whole in general and for nature in particular, including man.

Figure 6.2: Getting to the Core

Getting to real knowledge that is motivating and supportive of life means getting to the core assumptions that drive our cultures and worldviews. Bohm (2002) argues that there is a "hidden wholeness" in the universe that brings meaning, integrity, and complexity from relative disorder. The wholeness that can emerge is greater than the sum of its parts. Our core assumptions are life-giving only if they point to the greater wholeness.

In the example of the Good Samaritan, an unpredictable and transcending outcome emerged that changed the assumptions of the listeners. The story suggests that members of a tribe can truly love their enemies. The images and possibilities, once seen, serve to lure people toward a higher level of consciousness.

Bruce Sanguin (2012), an evolutionary theologian, says that the ordering and patterning of information in emergence influences reality toward greater unity, diversity, and consciousness by exerting an upward or forward pull. Sanguin imagines this as more than the push of the evolutionary impulse. *It's also an alluring pull from the future.* As Bohm also suggests, information exists in an implicit order, a realm of higher or greater possibility that influences the evolutionary processes. In creative emergence the wholeness in the universe, once revealed, can change our core assumptions.[25]

---

24 Snellman (2010) says that the knowledge we create is a "map" of reality; it is a representation of reality. Thus to claim there is "no meaning" in the universe or nature is to mistake a map for all reality.

25 Carter Phipps (2012) presents examples of visionary scientists, philosophers, and spiritual thinkers that are bringing about a new understanding of evolution that "honors science, reframes culture, and radically updates spirituality."

ARCHETYPAL PATTERNS

The patterns that emerge in creative emergence are a function of what is put into the mix: our worldview, our values, our cognitive abilities and capacity to find meaning.[26] The quality of the patterns we construct depends on what our ways of knowing contribute and the quality of our creative emergence processes. Inevitably, we see connections and combinations of larger patterns. Amidst the uncertainties of life we see periods of stability when the change processes slow down or even apparently stop. Taylor (2007) calls these emerging patterns "complex dynamic networks." He sees them as "subtly shifting pockets of stability in the midst of fluxes and flows (p. 347)[27]

The patterns that emerge are often linked to an archetype, an innate, inherited potential in our psyches that organize our thoughts, images, and observations (Jung, 1919). The content of these archetypal patterns are shaped by our history, culture, personal context, and our preferred ways of knowing. Jung described the archetype as representing fundamental human motifs of our experiences that developed and became inherent as we evolved as a species. Although there are many different archetypes, as individuals we tend to have several that dominate our personalities. Some common archetypal patterns include the hero, the caregiver, the explorer, the rebel, the creator, the jester, and the sage (figure 6.3). Whatever archetypes are present in each of us, they define our personas and our stories.

Figure 6.3 Archetype of the Hero

These archetypal patterns affect the way we interpret and re-produce ideas and behaviors. Every culture has archetypal patterns that affect the way inhabitants make sense of things. In the U.S.A. we prize "efficiency" and "activity," patterns helpful for economic success. We also like rounded numbers. In other societies, ghosts, gods, ancestor spirits, and dragons provide guidance (Sperber, in Brockman, pp. 180–183).

In creative emergence there is the opportunity to explore the patterns that have emerged from each of the four ways of knowing. This helps us understand the archetypal forces that are at work and gain more awareness and control of how they are affecting our lives.

When we create metaphors and stories that name these archetypal patterns, we create

---

26 Complexity scientists call these patterns "attractors," an image of an emergent behavior that has a finite boundary and infinite variability within the boundary.

27 Bob Luther, one of the readers, said this reminds him of the Jewish concept of Sabbath. Wholeness and health come with periods of rest.

hidden layers. This is how Wilczek (in Brockman, 2012, pp. 188–191) explains micro-evolution. As patterns form and reform, inevitably, small changes occur. As they are repeated, the changes are fed back on themselves, transferring meaning and causing the patterns to amplify and grow.

After several iterations, a small variance can cause enormous impact. The disparity between old and new archetypal patterns, their similarities and differences, are the sources of new tensions and new creative possibilities.

PURPOSE

Do we just imagine the purpose of events and observations (insight)? Do we think there is a purpose to life because it was created by our ancestors and handed down to us (authority)? Do the patterns that we perceive with our senses have an inherent purpose (empirical)? Do we create a purpose by being active in the world (praxis)? What if all are true? What if a super-purpose, a meta-purpose, arises from the zone of self-organizing creative emergence?

Each way of knowing serves some purpose. We would not have thrived as a species if we did not have all four modes of knowing. As a species, we have insights for a reason. There is an inherent purpose in our finding meaning in what we have been told by others (authority). The "facts" of empiricism do not speak for themselves. We ascribe purpose to them. We do not act (praxis) without some purpose. Each mode has an outcome that we construe as purposeful.

If purpose is present as we access each mode, what about its presence in the creative emergence process? Can our participation in creative emergence give us a better understanding of our place in the cosmos (figure 6.4)? Can we heal the rifts in our civilizations by transforming our awareness of our purpose?

In creative emergence there is a blend of openness balanced with constraint and the freedom associated with uncertainty that allows evolution to be purposive. Teilhard de Chardin (2008) argued that there is an "Omega Point" which draws our consciousness to a spiritual level.[28]

Creative emergence helps us to think of purpose as a reflective event. As we make meaning of things, it is like tracing one path (of many possible

Figure 6.4: Purpose

---

28 Davies (2004, pp. 95–96) believes that the very laws of nature that allow for radical chance to produce novel events suggests that there is an implicit teleology or purpose in nature, that is, that creation is moving toward a goal of self-realization. From this perspective, purpose is everywhere and in every particle, cell, compound, mass, and form of energy in the cosmos. The anthropic principle has even raised the serious consideration that the universe itself has a purpose, which is to support complex life (Sharpe and Walgate, 2002).

paths) through the branches and roots of a bush from an "alpha" to an "omega." Purpose, then, becomes an act of reflection upon changes occurring in time.[29]

As we integrate the ways of knowing we are able to navigate the complexities of modern life and discern what matters most to us and to others. Handy (1998) says that clarifying our purpose helps us to leave a legacy, proof that we made a difference to someone.

Purpose in life is recognition that one has—in both the past and future sense—important and socially useful work to perform. When individuals "find" a purpose for their lives, they discover the sense of aliveness and mattering to the world that comes from dedicating some portion of their lives to personally and socially important activities. With a purpose, individuals' futures remain important to them precisely because they have unfinished business to accomplish[30].

In 2010, neuropsychologist Patricia Boyle found that during up to seven years of follow-up, greater purpose in life was associated with a substantially reduced risk of Alzheimer's disease. A person with a high score on the purpose in life measure was over two times more likely to remain free of Alzheimer's disease than was a person with a low score.

Perhaps our *homo sapiens* species has survived and thrived because those persons selected in the evolutionary process had a sense of purpose greater than the other hominids.

IMPLICATIONS FOR ORGANIZATIONAL AND SOCIETAL ISSUES

We face situations at every level of society—individual, group, organization, community, nation, and global—where there is great disunity and inequity. We live in a culture where many people categorize their world-views in terms of simplistic dichotomies—red or blue states, scientific or religious, and socialist or capitalist. This compartmentalization interferes with our ability to deal with the ramification of realities that confront us on a daily basis.

Although the world is more interconnected through technology, the simplistic dichotomies in our politics, our religions, and our worldviews have prevented coordinated and collaborative responses to such crucial issues as climate change, hunger, and war. Our view of reality is partial. We are influenced by our methods for approaching reality, by our colleagues, by our prior views, our worldviews, and by our current interests and passions.

Knowledge and information is defined differently in religious traditions, academic

---

29 Thanks to James Reho for the bush metaphor of seeing purpose in reflections upon change occurring over time. For example, Barbara McClintock (Comfort, 2003) discovered that purposeful changes occur in genes. She says these changes occur as transposable elements, jump to specific places to insert themselves into genetic material, and alter it. She was the first to recognize that genes can repair themselves. She came to this understanding by developing what she called "a feeling for the organism."

30 Ryff (1989) points out that a mature person has a "clear comprehension of life's purpose, a sense of directedness, and intentionality." He says "one who functions positively has goals, intentions, and a sense of direction, all of which contribute to the feeling life is meaningful." Kekes (1995) says that two key developmental tasks for individuals, if they are to claim and pursue lives of purpose, are (1) to discern what are good or useful objectives in life, and (2) to successfully and ethically realize those ends in life. Both tasks are the underpinnings of wisdom.

disciplines, and in multiple worldviews. There are many theories, authorities, texts, experiences, and modes of analysis that vary by historical period, region, practices, doctrines, and beliefs.

The way we choose to know things shapes the way we see ourselves and the world we inhabit. We define ourselves and our relations with others by the questions we ask and how we consider the answers we receive. How we respond to life events depends on our level of confidence in our ways of knowing. Mark Twain said, "It ain't what you don't know that gets you into trouble. It's what you know for sure that just ain't so."[31]

To apply the Ways of Knowing Model to organizational and societal issues and avoid being certain about things "that just ain't so," it is helpful to generate questions using each way of knowing.

To illustrate, I have selected three organization and societal issues based on my own interest and background: moral leadership, religious organizations, and a global ethic. The Ways of Knowing Model could be applied to many other issues, including practical business issues. To emphasize this, the chapter ends with a case study that applies the Model to a start-up business organization.

Moral Leadership

O'Dea (2012) believes that the leaders of the future need more than "mentally focused intelligence" (p. 208). He says we need leaders who integrate the instinctual intelligence of the gut, the spacious inclusiveness of the heart, and the lucidity of the mind. He looks to these distributed intelligences in the body and new consciousness about human wholeness to go beyond reductionism and expand human capabilities. Moral leaders are motivated by a deep sense of ethics, ideals, and a higher purpose to serve and develop the capacities of others.

Using multiple ways of knowing, a moral leader can reconcile conflicting moral principles and duties to the multiple constituencies they serve.

Insight. A moral leader can ask, "What am I passionate about? What is my vision that will be compelling for others?"

Authority. What have I learned from the

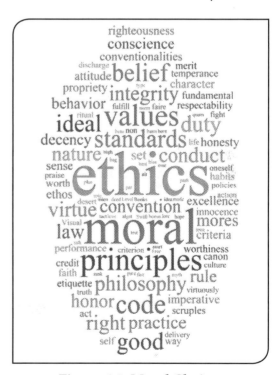

Figure 6.5: Moral Choices

---

31 Except it wasn't Twain after all. The quote was written by Charles F. Kettering in an article "Research and Industry", published in *Scientific American*, Volumes 156–157 (1937). This is just an example of how what we think we know for sure (who first turned a pithy phrase) may be something that just ain't so.

moral dilemmas I have faced that I need to pass on to others? How can I help others think through their purpose?

Empiricism. How much impact do the issues I focus on have on the human condition? How many people, cultures, races, etc., are involved? If the issues are ones important only to a small number, are there other issues on which I might focus? What information do we need?

Praxis. Have I shared what I know based on my life experiences? Do I practice hospitality, respect, humility, and other actions that demonstrate that I care? As I influence others, am I also influenced? Do I create space for others to speak their fears and uncertainties and build a sense of community?

RELIGIOUS ORGANIZATIONS

Religion-supporting organizations of all faiths are facing many challenges including losing membership, increased questioning of some long-held tenets, and attracting persons to fill leadership roles (both clergy and laity). Using all four ways of knowing can help these religious bodies be more relevant to the needs of their members and their surrounding communities.

Figure 6.6: Church Organizations and Their Symbols

Insight. Are the leaders willing to disrupt existing patterns through open conversations? Are personal stories told to provide new and novel viewpoints? Are important big questions being asked, such as who is God, what are human beings, how are we separated from the divine, what or who is the Spirit, what is religious organization, what should it be doing, and what is our hope for the future of the earth and humanity?

Authority. Are the answers provided to deep questions relevant for today? Are groups of people excluded? Are religion and science pitted against each other? Is theism presented as provisional, that is, that it represents only one particular expression of belief?

Empiricism. Is the theology coherent and relevant to the world today? Does it help members make sense of the world as revealed in nature? Does the conversation concern matters that are significant for both the members and the surrounding community?

Praxis. Does the mission include caring for the poor and oppressed, efforts to reconcile conflicts, and support of a sustainable environment? Is the organization willing to sacrifice for the persons outside its walls?

GLOBAL ETHIC

In the view of cultural anthropologists, unwritten ethical norms form the rock on which human society is built. One can call this a "primal ethic" that forms the core of a common ethic of humankind, a global ethic. Implementing a global ethic around such momentous issues as climate change is an enormous challenge. Looking at the reality of the issue from the perspective of the four ways of knowing will help.

Intuition. Do we think that humans are the crown of creation and that nature has only instrumental value? Do we need to change our assumptions about the inherent value of perpetual economic growth? Can we recapture a sense of the sacredness of creation and our responsibility as co-creators?

Authority. Can we create a global ethic that embraces diverse cultures, civilizations, and traditions that span the globe? Can it be continuously reinvented and projected? Can a moral code be developed that furthers the evolution of a sustainable balance of human activity and the flourishing of nature in our biosphere (Kauffman, p. 273)?

Figure 6.7: Global Ethic

Empiricism. "Keystone species are those that have a disproportionate effect relative to its abundance" (Brockman, 2012, p. 175). If a keystone species is removed from the environment, there is a sharp decline in diversity, many other species become extinct, and one species takes over. Can we protect keystone species and curb keystone consumption? Can we develop connections, networks, and niches to advance the long-term welfare of this planet and its inhabitants?

Praxis.

> *Thoreau and the Billerica Dam.* Salmon, shad, and alewives were formerly abundant here, and taken in weirs by the Indians ... until the dam and afterward the canal at Billerica, and the factories at Lowell, put an end to their migrations hitherward ... who knows what admirable virtue of fishes may be below low water-mark, bearing up against a hard destiny, not admired by the fellow creature who alone can appreciate it! Who hears the fishes when they cry?

> Henry David Thoreau, 1849

Society is entangled and interrelated in ways we barely comprehend. The impact of human decisions are felt by many stakeholders of whom we are not even aware, such as the shad that were under water when the Billerica Dam was built. Thoreau mourned their fate. Are we aware of our environmental impact? Who hears the fishes when they cry?

Can we identify the choices that perpetuate global warming and make new choices that will generate different responses? Can we develop practices that will connect us to the natural world? Can we find communities to build support systems to change how we are impacting the environment?

FLOAT MONEY, LLC

This case study shows how the Ways of Knowing Model can be used by a small group or team to explore a practical topic of strategic importance. I have used this approach to help a sales organization decide on whether to adopt a new product line, a church organization decide how to expand its membership, a non-profit group to improve customer satisfaction, and, in the case below, a finance company deciding on its marketing strategy.

The value of including all members of the team is to broaden and deepen team awareness of the topic by obtaining the perspective of each member on each of the four ways of knowing.

The Finance Case

Float Money, LLC, (Float) is a Lexington, Kentucky, based company dedicated to providing a new way people can develop credit and borrow money without having to pay interest (www.floatmoney.com). I met with the CEO, Shane Hadden, who had expressed an interest in the Ways of Knowing Model and wondered if it could be useful for his company.

Step 1: Deciding on a Focus

After considering several alternatives, Shane decided to focus on marketing their product and services, especially since on the following weekend the team would be headed to Atlanta to test a specific strategy with potential customers.

Step 2: Orient the Team

I met with Shane and his team of three and introduced the four ways of knowing. Shane introduced the topic for discussion and I reviewed this agenda.

1 Adaptive Action—What, So What, Now What?

2 Brainstorm: What we know

3 Interaction of ways of knowing

4 Emerging possibilities—So what?

5 Focus on one possibility—Now what?

6 Review self-assessments; process the session

7 End; next steps

Step 3: Team Brainstorm—Exploring the *What*

Each member of the team offered their thoughts or ideas about the topic from their perspective of each way of knowing. These thoughts were posted on a large whiteboard. These are the items grouped by the four ways of knowing:

Insight

People are curious; we need to be in the right location to meet the right people; we must be visually credible; first impressions are important; people may be defensive and emotional; they fear financial loss.

Authority

People believe that debt is bad (not safe) and leads to dangerous loans. They believe: "I must be responsible;" they distrust lenders; celebrity advisers such as Dave Ramsey are influential.

Empiricism

We have data about the impact of debt and credit scores; short-term debt becomes long-term debt; people are over confident, disconnected from reality; the economy is down – cost outpaces wages; people don't like to talk about finances.

Praxis

Some people listen, some find a "bucket" for it and stop listening; I can share my story and experience; people like giveaways, it will get their attention; people are either open or closed; the environment must be conducive.

Step 4: Creative Emergence—Identify the *So What*

The team was asked to let their collective knowledge from each mode of knowing interact with the other modes. These are the results:

Insight and Authority

Location and signage will determine what people believe and the kinds of defenses they have. We must show we are different from traditional lenders.

Authority and Empiricism

We agree that debt can be bad, but the debt you create with Float is "safe" (like a Volvo). There are new options that will inform what you think. We need to develop our own authority through endorsements.

Empiricism and Praxis

We have a new model that replaces interest-based lending. We need a visual device to show how what is borrowed is replaced. We need to help them to forget what they "know." We need to create an easy way to try it out.

Praxis and Insight

Banners and T-shirts to appeal to the "common man." Be interactive with customers with games and prizes. Qualify the customer.

Step 5: Team Analysis of what Emerged—Planning the *Now What*

Shane led a discussion to develop specific next steps based on the following key emergent ideas.

- Use the Ways of Knowing Model to identify the "hot buttons" to make a sale.
- Develop a script that is appropriate for each type of customer. If the customer values:
    ◦ insight, then use words like new, innovative, safe.
    ◦ authority, then lead with endorsements.
    ◦ empiricism, then lead with data.
    ◦ praxis, lead with an exercise like finding their potential interest-free credit line.
- Create an "aha" moment.

Reflection on the Process at Float Money, LLC

The process allowed each team member to give voice to their thoughts. One new member of the team, who initially was reluctant to share her insights because of her usual deference to authority, discovered how important her ideas were for the team. By the end of the session the team not only realized the value of analysis by the four ways of knowing, but even began to frame their strategy using the model.

The analysis using the Ways of Knowing Model (WOK) has helped Shane and his team clarify their direction in relation to customer acquisition. As they reflected on the analysis, they realized that empiricism and insight are strong points for them. Their data clearly show that people know that interest can be dangerous and people intuitively feel bad owing compounding interest. Praxis is also on their side since when people try Float, they like it. Their problem in acquiring customers is with authority since the high profile advisers and the credit card industry create their own form of authority through advertising. The team determined that their strategy should be focused on (1) gaining acceptance and an endorsement from one or more high-profile advisers and (2) countering the "cult" of the credit card through blogs, word of mouth, and humor. Shane said:

> Prior to this I knew "trust" was an issue, but with the benefit of WOK I can
> see clearly that if we turn authority from a negative to a positive, we will then

have a very clear path using the other three ways of knowing to make the sale. Authority is currently the roadblock that we have to get through.

The Model was useful for the team's exploration of the topic, for assessing their own preferred ways of knowing, and, perhaps most importantly, the ways of knowing of their potential customers.

SUMMARY

A useful epistemology for our times makes us more aware of how our worldview provides a lens through which we "know" reality. There may be other lenses not valued by our worldview that will help us.

The creative emergence of the interaction of the four ways of knowing is one way of looking at this expanding human consciousness. Integrating or transcending polarities of competition/cooperation, the self/group, part/whole, and finite/infinite are possible with the container of creative emergence.

The Ways of Knowing Model can be used to transform our core assumptions into a holistic perspective that is life-giving, gain more control over the archetypal patterns that influence us, develop a greater sense of our purpose in the world, deepen our understanding of important organizational and societal issues, and deal with everyday practical problems.

QUESTIONS FOR REFLECTION

1. Reflect on which archetypal pattern is dominant in your life, e.g., "I always want to be the hero," I always want to take care of others," "I always like to be in control," or "I always like to make jokes." What does each way of knowing say to your pattern? The results may diminish the power of the archetype or put it in perspective with the other stories that you are living.

2. Do you believe your life has a purpose? Is there an inherent purpose in the universe? Does tapping into the wisdom of all four ways of knowing help you answer these questions?

POSSIBLE ACTIONS

1. Identify one of your core assumptions. What challenge is presented by each of the four ways of knowing? Ask someone to be an advocate for each way of knowing and engage in dialogue. The outcome of the dialogue may strengthen your core assumptions, modify them, or replace them with others.

2. Choose an important environmental issue and use the Ways of Knowing Model to start a dialogue with others. You can ask

   • what is happening here to individuals, groups, and communities in this moment?

   • so what are my options for action to meet my responsibility to support health and sustainability in the biosphere?

   • now what will I do, in this moment, to influence patterns that improve the present and contribute to a fruitful future for all species?

3. Identify a specific practical issue that could be usefully explored in a group or team. Use the five steps in the Float Money, LLC, case to facilitate a discussion using the four ways of knowing.

Workbooks for Finding Reality!!
Workbooks and study guides based on the Ways of Knowing and Adaptive Action Models are being developed for specific readers including:
   Personal and professional development
   Teams and groups
   Organizations
Further information is available at www.findingreality.net

Appendix A:
The CDE Model and Ways of Knowing

U sing the CDE Model of self-organizing (figure A.1) we can adjust our use of the four modes.

THE CDE MODEL

The CDE Model has been shown to be a powerful method for both diagnosing and intervening in human systems and addressing real world problems.

The CDE model identifies the three conditions that influence our use of the four ways of knowing.[32] They are the containers, differences, and exchanges.

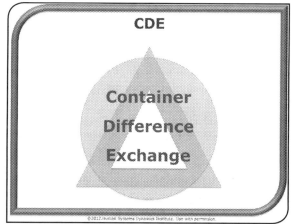

Figure A.1: CDE Model

Container (C)

Containers hold our perceptive and meaning-making processes together. This holding-together condition is called a *container* and is represented by *C* in the model. What holds things together may be an idea, a goal, a closed room, a national boundary, a time period, an organization chart, a shared language, or any other physical, emotional, social, political, or conceptual feature.

For example, the containers in our Apollo 13 story included the lunar modules, the Houston team, the hope that they could create a miracle, the lithium hydroxide canisters, and the reality that they could only work with what the astronauts had available. If the container is too small, tight, and constrained, our use of the mode is limited. If the container is too large, loose, and unconstrained, our use of the mode will not have enough clarity and focus.

It is necessary to strike a balance between strong and weak constraints in a container

---

32 Ursula Goodenough (1998, p. 38) describes the basic processes of life—how our cells, the building blocks of life, use enzymes in our body. Her description illustrates the CDE model very well. Enzymes are the proteins in our cells that have pockets. The pockets bring small molecules of sugar together to form a chemical bond between them. In this analogy, the enzyme is a small container within the larger container of the cell. The two different sugar molecules are the significant difference. The action of the enzyme to bring the two molecules together is the exchange that transforms. This process at the center of the creation of life suggests how the CDE process works at all scales and levels in the application of the ways of knowing.

for novelty and creativity to emerge. Too much constraint makes it difficult for the modes to interact. Too little constraint makes it difficult to have meaningful contact[33] between the modes. If we influence the container, we influence the way the modes interact.

Bruce Sanguin (March, 2014) has pointed out that a holding environment for the self is a container, actually a containing process for each stage of our development. The three functions of a holding container are (1) to hold, signaling to us that it is a safe place; (2) to let go, when we are ready to let go to move to the next stage; and (3) to challenge us if we are lingering and not moving on. Under stress we default to the holding environment in our development that was not good enough. This is also true on a collective level. The worldviews are holding environments, representing different intelligences, different ways of knowing, that routinely privilege the status quo.

Difference (D)

The ways of knowing have to contain significant differences or no new knowledge will emerge. This condition is called *difference* and is represented by a *D*. Significant differences can appear in any of the modes, for example, new insights, new scientific discoveries, new hypotheses, or new instances of trial and error. Significant differences may appear in conflicting or dangerous situations.

For example, in the Apollo 13 story the significant differences included the MER team and Don Arabian's knowledge, the available material (e.g. duct tape), and unsafe CO_2 levels. Differences we pay attention to determine the outcome of our use of the mode. If there are too many differences, it is difficult to discern new knowledge. If there is not enough significant difference, we continue with our usual patterns of knowing and the usual outcomes.

Exchange (E)

When a way of knowing makes contact across the significant difference, situations are transformed. This condition is called *exchange*, represented by *E* in the model. An exchange is a connection that transmits information, resources, or energy within or between the ways of knowing.

For example, in the Apollo 13 story the exchanges included discussions with the MER team, experiments with the material in the simulator, and communications between the astronauts and Houston.

When one mode receives an exchange, the dynamics in the mode are changed. When the mode changes, it transmits information, resources, or energy to other ways of knowing that receive it and are themselves changed.

If the exchanges are too strong and one-sided they dominate the interaction and new

---

33   In Gestalt psychology, *contact* is the awareness of the meeting of differences. Contact occurs at the boundary of one aspect of the self with another aspect or with some aspect in the environment. If the contact is genuine, within the moment of contact all else merges to the background; both aspects are changed.

knowledge will not emerge; we remain stuck. If the exchange is too weak, any new knowledge will dissipate and we are left with the status quo. Many conflicts are rooted in a weak exchange of information.

For example, technology has shifted exchanges between the modes. Exchanges by email are weaker than face-to-face exchanges, but social networks now allow wider patterns of exchange. With each change some people benefit and some are disadvantaged, e.g. online commerce and the decline of the local retailer (Eoyang and Holladay, 2013).

Summary of CDE Model

Container, difference, and exchange are the conditions that influence how we use the ways of knowing and how clear and how close to reality the resulting knowledge will be. Each of our modes may be too constrained or too unconstrained. We can ask if our containers need to be loosened or tightened. We can see if we are focused on the significant difference—does it matter? We can change our exchanges across the modes of knowing. We can make them longer, deeper, broader, or narrower.

Engaging with the other modes can help achieve the appropriate balance of constraint. Any changes we make will affect the self-organizing conditions of Container, Difference, and Exchange. The good news is that by changing only one of the conditions in one of the modes we can have an impact on the others.

Glossary

This is a list of some of the concepts about ways of knowing and the complexity sciences as used in this book that differ, at least in part, from those used in conventional conversation.

Adaptive Action

Plan of action wherein you cannot predict or control what will happen. This allows action to fit the situation at hand. The three actions are (1) collect data and observe environment (what); (2) make sense of information (so what); and (3) take adaptive action *now* (now what).

Adjacent possible

Kauffman (2008) describes how biological species keep jumping into what is adjacent to them and what is possible. In doing so they increase the diversity of what can happen next. It is a metaphor for thinking about what actions we can take in response to new opportunities.

Amplify

To focus on or provide positive feedback about behavior to assure the continuation of a particular behavior

Ascribed Meaning

Ascribed meaning is the belief that something is meaningful based on the intuition and empirical investigations of others—authority figures, written records, persons we have met, read about, or heard of.

Attractors

In complex systems theory, an attractor is the physical aspect toward or around which elements of the system are drawn to create an attractor pattern.

Attractor Patterns

System-wide patterns that emerge as self-organizing change progresses. There are four classes of attractor patterns: (1) random—no discernible pattern; (2) point—all in system moves toward single point; (3) periodic—cyclical pattern returning to beginning; (4) strange—finite boundary, infinite options in coherent pattern. Which patterns actually emerge over time will depend upon both the initial configuration and the subsequent perturbations.

Authority

Authority is one of the four modes of knowing. In our quest to understand the unknowns, along with others we developed theories and beliefs to explain the mysterious phenomena we experience in places, objects, persons, rituals, times, and stories. This knowledge may be expressed as conventional wisdom, ethics, and moral knowledge that are organized around and relied on commonly accepted *external* authorities (codes, scriptures, laws) or people. In more recent times there has been a shift to organizing around and relying on *internal* authority.

Boundaries

Boundaries separate systems from their external environment and internal sub-units from each other. It is where differences meet, generating learning and growth, or conflict and disruption. Differences can concern demography, expertise, discipline, role, power, location, etc. System boundaries are neither closed nor totally open.

CDE Model

The three conditions that influence the path, speed, and outcomes of self-organizing processes in systems (container, difference, and exchange). Formulated by Glenda H. Eoyang (2001) and applied in Olson and Eoyang (2001) and Eoyang and Holladay (2013).

Conditions of Self-Organization

Complex systems dynamics consist of patterns that are produced by the interaction of three conditions or forces—containing, differentiating, and connecting. If any of the three conditions change, the patterns change. Containers hold the system together. The differences differentiate the part from the whole and connections are how the parts contact and interact. We act on the patterns that we see. Behavior, emotions, and belief systems all have the three conditions embedded.

Constraints

System patterns that limit or influence the behaviors of the agents in a system. Constraints are factors that limit a condition of self-organizing or a mode of knowing. *Under-constrained* describes a situation in which there is not enough constraint to allow new patterns to form. *Over-constrained* describes a situation in which there is so much constraint on a condition or a mode of knowing that it is difficult for change to occur.

Container

Containers hold our perceptive and meaning-making processes together. What holds the processes together may be an idea, a goal, a closed room, a national boundary, a time period, an organization chart, a shared language, or any other physical, emotional, social, political, or conceptual feature. Containers set the bounds for the self-organizing system and define the pattern that organizes.

Creative Emergence

A self-organizing space in which the information from the ways of knowing blend and become a singularity. The person experiencing creative emergence reveals the pattern or order that emerges. Whether a person is a writer, artist, dancer, worker, student, etc., the order becomes visible and accessible as the ways of knowing merge and the person acts on them. The new knowledge flows through that person, not from him or her. The person records the process of experienced creative emergence.

Difference (Significant Differences)

Variances that emerge during self-organizing processes that are reflected and reinforced by other agents in the system to establish a new system-wide pattern.

Dominant Mode

In the Ways of Knowing Model, a mode of knowing that is so preferred that it may limit the use of the other three modes.

Downward Causation

A condition in which the properties of the whole system affect the existence and properties of the parts. This forms constraints on the freedom of the parts. For example, we humans determine the fate of our cells by our actions as much as their interactions determine us. Think of the positive impact on our cells when we participate in fitness programs.

Dynamical Change

In *dynamical* change the factors involved in a change process are too great to meaningfully identify and ultimately unknowable so that it is impossible to predict effects and outcomes. This is contrasted to *static* change, which focuses on moving from one place or state to another when we have control over all of the significant variables, and *dynamic* change, in which most of the variables are knowable, predictable, and controllable to a sufficient degree to accomplish intended results (Eoyang & Holladay, pp. 62–64).

Emergence

Emergence is the unpredictable result of the new combination of forces and materials without direct, linear action. System properties are not describable in terms of their parts. Emergence deals with the opportunities and challenges that arise in the context of complex relationships among the parts of a system.

Emergent

Emergent is a coming into existence. It may be a property, action, or process.

Empiricism

Empiricism is a way of knowing what represents objective reality and truth as verified by evidence.

Epistemology

Epistemology is the philosophy of the grounds of knowledge, including its limits and validity.

Exchanges (Transforming Exchanges)

These are the transfer of material, energy, or information between parts of a system that transforms each part in some way, leading to adaptability of the system as a whole.

Exemplars

An exemplar is an ideal example of something worthy of being copied or imitated. In this book several human exemplars have been identified.

Experienced Meaning

Experienced meaning is our awareness that something is meaningful because our personal experiences observed through our senses and intuition proves it to our satisfaction.

Far from Equilibrium

When a system dissipates energy and information, disorder is created, leading ultimately to some new, unpredictable order rather than a return to the previous equilibrium.

Feedback Loops

When the outputs of a process are fed back into the beginning of the process they can affect the inputs to the process. Uncertainty is caused if there are not feedback loops to inform about the impact of the process. The loops vary in length, width, and duration (Olson & Eoyang, pp. 40–44).

Generative Emergence

In generative emergence, the emergent property or action is intentional. The emergence is initiated by a desire, goal, passion, opportunity, or an aspiration to affect the situation in some specific way. The original direction is never the end result because of the dynamics of feedback and experimentation that happens in emergence (Lichtenstein, 2014)

Holistic

Holism is a focus on whole systems rather than the parts or a particular focus. It is the opposite of "reductive."

Human Systems Dynamics (HSD)

The ongoing study of the complexities inherent in day-to-day interactions of individuals who work or live together as a self-organizing system. HSD is an integrating, embracing field developed by Glenda H. Eoyang that brings together complexity theory and practice from diverse disciplines and applies it to what happens within and among human beings in organizations and communities from local to global levels.

Idolatry

Idolatry is the devotion to something or worship of a physical object as a god. In this book it is argued, along with Barfield (1965), that using only one or two of the ways of knowing may be idolatrous.

Insight

Insight is a way of knowing what combines our intuitive way of perceiving things and our ability to make meaning through our personal experience. This way of knowing includes (1) our ability to pre-understand something we may later be able to know theoretically and (2) our ability to sense "something more" that is beyond words and indescribable by our senses.

Intuition

Intuition does not depend on or arise from the five senses. It is the realm of the unconscious, dreams, flashes of insight, the unmanifest, the unseen, and the unfathomable dimension of reality. We experience intuition when we let go of thought, feeling, and time—a static and unchanging, beginingless and endless, timeless and formless dimension. Intuition and senses are the two aspects of perception.

Meaning

Meaning is a dimension of the Ways of Knowing Model. *Meaning* is how we use both our experience (experienced meaning) and what others have told us (ascribed meaning) to understand what our senses and our intuitions tell us. This dimension was derived from the concepts of ascribed and experienced coherence by Letiche, Lissack, and Schultz (2011). Meaning is an emergent property. It stands for what is intended to be or actually is expressed, communicated, or indicated. It may be about the end, purpose, or significance of something.

Modes of Knowing

See "Ways of Knowing"

Omega Point

Teilhard de Chardin (2008) argued that there is an "Omega Point" in creation which draws (or lures) our consciousness to a spiritual level.

Paradigms

A paradigm is a cognitive framework that is commonly accepted by members of a group, discipline, community, or society. A paradigm contains basic assumptions, ways of knowing, and methodology that influence behavior in the systems.

Patterns

Similarities, differences, and relationships that have meaning across space and time.

Perception

Perception is a dimension of the Ways of Knowing Model. It includes how we know things using our five senses (senses) and knowing something beyond our five senses (intuition). This dimension is similar to Carl Jung's description of the perceiving function which includes intuition (N) and sensing (S).

Praxis

Praxis is one of the four ways of knowing. It is our experienced coherence of knowing through acting on our understanding and inner sensation of who and how we are and why we are here. In praxis we enact, practice, and embody a theory or lesson. Ideas and skills are engaged, applied, and realized in praxis.

Proprioception

Proprioception is the unconscious perception of movement and spatial orientation arising from stimuli within the body itself. In humans, these stimuli are detected by nerves within the body, as well as by the semicircular canals of the inner ear. Retrieved from www.prescriptionputting.com, June 2014.

Purpose

Purpose is "the reason why something is done or used; the aim or intention of something; the feeling of being determined to do or achieve something; the aim or goal of a person; what a person is trying to do, become, etc." Retrieved from http://www.merriam-webster.com/dictionary/purpose, July 3, 2014.

Reality

Reality is a framework in which people organize their beliefs around axioms that are contained in the worldviews they have inherited (McIntosh, 2012).

Reductionism, Reductive

In the process of knowing, an extreme focus on one way of knowing that denies the value and contribution of the other ways of knowing. In systems this is the separation of components into constituents with the notion that the whole is not greater than its parts.

Resilience

Resilience is "the ability to become strong, healthy, or successful again after something bad happens; the ability of something to return to its original shape after it has been pulled, stretched, pressed, bent, etc." Retrieved from http://www.merriam-webster.com/dictionary/resilience?show=0&t=1404517757, July 2014.

Self-Organization

When conditions are right, order is created within a system. A system that is pushed far-from-equilibrium restructures itself. We can influence, but not control, self-organizing processes. The amount of time it takes to self-organize is unpredictable. Self-organization requires appropriate conditions of containing, difference, and exchange.

Self-Organized Criticality

Self-organized criticality refers to the way in which internal dynamics can result in unpredictable system-wide transformations. Self-organizing systems exhibit order and stay stable for a long time and then change dramatically. Gladwell (2002) popularized the notion as the "tipping point."

Sensing

One of the two functions of perception. It includes how we know things using our five senses of touch, taste, sight, hearing, and smell.

Sensitive to Initial Conditions

Small causes or fluctuations can have a huge, unpredictable effect in systems poised far from equilibrium. Known as the "butterfly effect," related to tipping point. This can also work in the negative when apparently large causes have little effect.

Socially Constructed Reality

According to Berger and Luckmann (1966), society is constructed through three stages: (1) creation of cultural products through social interaction; (2) products created in the first stage appear to take on a reality of their own, becoming independent of those who created them; (3) we learn the "objective facts" about the cultural products that have been created without much explanation. These three stages create strong beliefs about things by internalizing the social constructs as the "proper" way to behave.

Technium

Kevin Kelly (2010) calls the technium, "The current physical accumulation of all that humans have created, the sphere of visible technology and organizations that form modern culture."

Tipping Point

See "Self-organized Criticality"

Truth

Four kinds of truth: objective (evidence); subjective (what I believe to be true based on my experience); normative (what we agree to be true); pragmatic (what works).

Uncertainty

Basic assumptions shift in times of complex change and previous predictions no longer hold true. The initial conditions in a complex adaptive system can create radical uncertainty.

Ways of Knowing

The ways (modes) of knowing represent reality and truth, albeit from different sources. *Insight* represents subjective reality and the truth of individuals. *Authority* represents normative reality and the truths of a collective of people. *Empiricism* represents objective reality and truth as verified by evidence. *Praxis* represents practical reality and personally integrated truth. All four modes are valuable and necessary for life, but it is from their interaction that deeper levels of knowledge emerge.

Wisdom

Wisdom is the quality or state of being wise, knowing what is true or right coupled with just judgment as to action. It usually implies scholarly knowledge, learning, wise sayings, or teachings. Matthew Fox (1988) says wisdom is always taste—in both Latin and Hebrew, the word for wisdom comes from the word for taste—so it is something to taste, not something to theorize about.

Bibliography

Avery, S. (2011). *Buddha and the Quantum: Hearing the Voice of Every Cell.* Boulder, CO: Sentient Publications. ISBN 978-159181106-0.

Axelrod, D. & E. Axelrod (2014). *Let's Stop Meeting Like This: Tools to Save Time and Get More Done.* San Francisco: Berrett-Koehler. ISBN 978-1-62656-081-9.

Barfield, O. (1965). *Saving Appearances: A Study in Idolatry.* Middletown, CT: Wesleyan University Press. ISBN 0-8195-6205-X.

Bell, R. (2013). *What We Talk About When We Talk About God.* New York: HarperOne. ISBN 13: 978-0062049667.

Berger, Peter L. and Thomas Luckmann (1966). *The Social Construction of Reality.* Garden City, NJ: Anchor Books.

Bohm, D. (2002). *Wholeness and the Implicate Order.* London: Routledge. ISBN 10: 0415289793.

Boyle, P.A., Buchman A.S., Barnes L.L., & Bennett, D.A. (2010, Mar.). "Effect of a Purpose in Life on Risk of Incident Alzheimer's Disease and Mild Cognitive Impairment in Community-Dwelling Older Persons." *Archives of General Psychiatry.* 67(3), 304–310.

Brady, J. (2011). "Cooking as Inquiry: A Method to Stir up Prevailing Ways of Knowing Food, Body, and Identity." *International Journal of Qualitative Methods.* 321–334.

Brockman, J. (2012). *This Will Make You Smarter: New Scientific Concepts to Improve Your Thinking.* New York: Harper Perennial. ISBN 13: 978-0062109392.

Cohen, A. & Chopra, D. (2011). *Evolutionary Enlightenment: A New Path to Spiritual Awakening.* N.Y.: SelectBooks. ISBN 1-59079-209-2.

Comfort, N.C. (2003). *The Tangled Field: Barbara McClintock's Search for the Patterns of Genetic Control.* Cambridge, MA: Harvard University Press.

Cox, H. (2009). *The Future of Faith.* New York: HarperOne. ISBN 978-0-06-1755521.

Davies, P. (2004). "Teleology Without Teleology: Purpose through Emergent Complexity." In P. Clayton, A. Peacocke and W. B. (Eds.), *In Whom We Live and Move and Have Our Being*, Grand Rapids: MI: Eerdmans. 95-108.

de Chardin, T. (2008). *The Phenomenon of Man*. New York: Harper.

Dew, J.K., Jr. & Foreman, M.W. (2014). *How Do We Know? An Introduction to Epistemology*. Wheaton, IL: IVP Academic. ISBN 978-0-8308-4036-6.

Dowd, M. (2008). *Thank God for Evolution*. New York: Viking. ISBN 978-0-670-02048-4.

Einstein, A. (1949). "Cosmic Religion: With Other Opinions and Aphorisms." *The World as I See It*. New York: Philosophical Library, 24–28.

Eoyang, G.H. (2001). "Conditions for Self-Organizing Systems." (unpublished dissertation, Union Institute and University).

Eoyang, G.H. & R. J. Holladay (2013). *Adaptive Action: Leveraging Uncertainty in Your Organization*. Stanford, CA: Stanford Business Books. ISBN:10:0-8047-8711-5.

Evers, D., Jackelén, A., & Smedes, T.A. (2010). *How Do We Know? Understanding in Science and Theology*. N.Y.: T&T Clark, Inc. ISBN: 978-0-567-13265-9.

Fox, M. (1988). *The Coming of the Cosmic Christ*. New York: Harper & Row. ISBN 0-06-062915-0.

Frank, A. (2010). *The Constant Fire: Beyond the Science vs. Religion Debate*. Berkeley, CA: University of California Press.

Frank, P. (1948). *Einstein: His Life and Times*. Ch. sct.5. London: Jonathan Cape.

Frankl, V. (2006). *Man and the Search for Meaning*. Boston: Beacon Press.

Gladwell, M. (2002). *The Tipping Point: How Little Things Can Make a Big Difference*. New York: Backbay Books.

Goodenough, U. (1998). *The Sacred Depths of Nature*. London: Oxford University Press. ISBN 978-0-19-513629-1.

Handy, C. (1998). *The Hungry Spirit: Beyond Capitalism: A Quest for Purpose in the Modern World*. New York: Broadway Books. ISBN 0-7679-0187-8.

Hobbes, T. (2013). *Leviathan*. Milwaukee, WI: Renaissance Books. Originally published 1660.

Hoeller, S.A. (2002). *Gnosticism: New Light on the Ancient Tradition of Inner Knowing.* Wheaton, IL: Quest Books. ISBN-10: 0835608166.

Holloway, R. (2003). "The Danger of Sincere Religion." Sermon. St Mark's Church, Sheffield, UK. http://homepages.which.net/~radical.faith/holloway/sermondangers.htm.

Jeeves, M & W.S. Brown (2009). *Neuroscience, Psychology, and Religion: Illusions, Delusions, and Realities About Human Nature.* West Conshohocken, PA: Templeton Foundation Press. ISBN 10:1-59947-147-7

Jinkins, M. (February 2014). "Durable Ideas. Thinking Out Loud." Blog by Jinkins, President of Louisville Seminary.

Jung, C.G. (1981). *The Archetypes and the Collective Unconscious, Collected Works* 9 (1) (2 ed.), Princeton, NJ: Bollingen. Originally published 1919. ISBN 0-691-01833-2.

Jung, C.G. (1981). *Psychological Types, Collected Works* 9 (1) (2 ed.), Princeton, NJ: Bollingen Originally published 1921. ISBN 0-691-01833-2.

Kauffman, S.A. (2008). *Reinventing the Sacred: A New View of Science, Reason, and Religion.* New York: Basic Books. ISBN 0465003001.

Kegan, R. (1982). *The Evolving Self: Problem and Process in Human Development.* Cambridge, MA: Harvard University Press. ISBN 0674272315.

Kegan, R. (1994). *In over Our Heads: The Mental Demands of Modern Life.* Cambridge, MA: Harvard University Press. ISBN 0674445880.

Kekes, J. (1995). *Moral Wisdom and Good Lives.* Ithaca, NY: Cornell University Press.

Kelly, K. (2010). *What Technology Wants.* New York: Viking. ISBN 978-0-670-02215-1.

Kettering, C.F. (1937). "Research and Industry." *Scientific American.* 156-157.

Klein, R.A. (2010). How Do We Know about the Self: Theoretical, Experimental, and Neural? in Evers, op. cit. pp 59–64.

Kluger, J & J. Lovell (1994). *Lost Moon: The Perilous Voyage of Apollo 13.* New York: Houghton Mifflin. ISBN-10: 0395670293.

Letiche, H., Lissack, M., & Schultz, R. (2011). *Coherence in the Midst of Complexity: Advances in Social Complexity Theory.* New York: Palgrave Macmillan. ISBN 978-0-230-33850-0.

Lewes, G.H. (1875). *Problems of Life and Mind (First series)* London: Trübner. ISBN 1-4255-5578-0.

Lichtenstein, B. (2014). *Generative Emergence: A New Science of Organizational, Entrepreneurial and Social Creation.* New York: Oxford University Press.

Loomis, M.E. (1991). *Dancing the Wheel of Psychological Types.* Asheville, NC: Chiron Publications. ISBN-10: 0933029497.

McIntosh, S. (2012). *Evolution's Purpose: An Integral Interpretation of the Scientific Story of Our Origins.* New York: SelectBooks. ISBN 978-1-59079-220-9.

Mitchell, M. (2009). *Complexity: A Guided Tour.* New York: Oxford. ISBN: 978-0-19-512441-5.

Morin, D., A. & Montuori, A (2008). *On Complexity.* New York: Hampton Press. ISBN 10: 1572738014.

Nolan, A. (2006). *Jesus Today: A Spirituality of Radical Freedom.* Maryknoll, NY: Orbis.

O'Dea, J (2012). *Cultivating Peace: Becoming a 21st-Century Peace Ambassador.* Chicago: Shift Books. ISBN-10: 0984840710.

Olson, E.E. (1990). "The Transcendent Function in Organizational Change." *Journal of Applied Behavioral Science.* ISSN 0021-8863, 26(1): 69–81.

Olson, E.E. & Eoyang, G.H. (2001). *Facilitating Organization Change: Lessons from Complexity Science.* San Francisco: Jossey-Bass/Pfeiffer. ISBN 078795330X.

Olson, E.E. (2009). *Keep the Bathwater: Emergence of the Sacred in Science and Religion.* Estero, FL: Island Sound Press. ISBN 0615275206.

Otto, R (1970). *The Idea of the Holy,* trans J.W. Harvey. New York: OUP, 1923; 2nd edn, 1950; reprint, 1970. ISBN 0-19-500210-5. Originally published 1917.

Peterson, E. (2011). *The Message.* Colorado Springs, CO: NavPress. ISBN-10: 1617479497.

Phipps, C. (2012). *Evolutionaries: Unlocking the Spiritual and Cultural Potential of Science's Greatest Idea.* New York: Harper. ISBN 978-0-06-191613-7.

Piety, M.G. (2010). *Ways of Knowing: Kierkegaard's Pluralist Epistemology.* Waco, TX: Baylor University Press.

Pinker, S. (1997). *How the Mind Works*. New York: Norton. ISBN 0-393-04535-8.

Pinson, P. (Fall, 2012). "Ways of Knowing in Walter Anderson." *Southern Quarterly*. University of Southern Mississippi. Vol. no 1. 167–195.

Reho, J. (Winter, 2013-14). "Liberating God from Heaven." *Parabola*. 84–93.

Ryff, C.D. (1989). "Happiness is Everything, or Is It? Explorations on the Meaning of Psychological Well-Being." *Journal of Personality and Social Psychology*, 57: 1069–1081.

Sanguin, B. (2008). *The Emerging Church*. Kelowna, BC: Copper House.

Sanguin, B. (2012). *The Advance of Love: Reading the Bible With an Evolutionary Heart*. Victoria, BC: Evans and Sanguin Publishing. ISBN 978-0-9865924-3-0.

Sanguin, B. (February 2014). "Raising the bar on church 'community'." Blog. Brucesanguin.com.,

Scott, B.B. (2001). *Re-Imagine the World: An Introduction to the Parables of Jesus*. Salem, OR: Polebridge Press.

Semmelweis, I. (1983). *Etiology, Concept and Prophylaxis of Childbed Fever*. Madison, WI: University of Wisconsin Press. ISBN 0-299-09364-6. Originally published 1861.

Sharpe, K. and Walgate, J. (2002). "The Anthropic Principle: Life in the Universe." *Zygon: Journal of Religion and Science*, 37: 925–939.

Sinclair, M. (2004). "Nietzsche and the Problem of History." *Richmond Journal of Philosophy*. 1–6.

Snellman, H. (2010). "The Scientific Project: Knowledge Without Meaning?" In Evers, op cit. pp. 45–58.

Snowber, C. (Summer, 2012). "Dance As a Way of Knowing." *New Directions for Adult and Continuing Education*, 2012(134), 53–60. DOI: 10.1002/ace.20017.

Sperber, D. (2012). Cultural Attractors." in Brockman, op. cit, pp. 180–183.

Taylor, M.C. (2007). *After God*. Chicago: University of Chicago Press. ISBN: 978-0-226-79171-5.

Thielicke, H. (1960). *The Waiting Father: Sermons on the Parables of Jesus*. Cambridge, England: James Clarke.

Thoreau, H.D. (2004). *A Week on the Concord and Merrimack Rivers*. Princeton, NJ: Princeton University Press. ISBN: 9780691118789. Originally published 1849.

Weick, K.E. (1995). *Sensemaking in Organizations.* Thousand Oaks, CA: Sage Publications.

Wjlezek, F. (2012). "Hidden Layers." in Brockman, op. cit., pp. 192–193.

Wolpert, L. & C. Tickle (2010). *Principles of Development.* New York: Oxford University Press.

Index

About the Author

Ed Olson is a collegiate professor at the University of Maryland, University College. He is a member of the NTL Institute of Applied Behavioral Science, a National Certified Counselor, and formerly an organization and management development consultant to many companies and government agencies.

Ed has a BA in Philosophy from St. Olaf College, an MS in Pastoral Counseling from Loyola College, and a PhD in Government and Public Administration from The American University. He writes and leads workshops that use complexity theory and archetypal psychology to explore issues in the management of organizations and the relationship of science, spirituality, and religion.

Ed is the author of *Facilitating Organization Change: Lessons from Complexity Science* (with Glenda Eoyang, 2001), *Keep the Bathwater: Emergence of the Sacred in Science and Religion,* (2009), and numerous papers and presentations at international conferences.

Ed has been married fifty-five years to Judith. They live in Estero, Florida, and have four children and eight grandchildren.